MW00960866

Dr Millican,
I am forever grateful.
Julie

Mediocre

Making Fun of Life

Julie McCulloch Burton

iUniverse, Inc.
Bloomington

30/30

Mediocre
Making Fun of Life

Copyright © 2013 Julie McCulloch Burton

All rights reserved. No part of this book may be used or reproduced by any means, graphic, electronic, or mechanical, including photocopying, recording, taping or by any information storage retrieval system without the written permission of the publisher except in the case of brief quotations embodied in critical articles and reviews.

iUniverse books may be ordered through booksellers or by contacting:

iUniverse
1663 Liberty Drive
Bloomington, IN 47403
www.iuniverse.com
1-800-Authors (1-800-288-4677)

Because of the dynamic nature of the Internet, any Web addresses or links contained in this book may have changed since publication and may no longer be valid. The views expressed in this work are solely those of the author and do not necessarily reflect the views of the publisher, and the publisher hereby disclaims any responsibility for them.

Photo credits: The cover photograph and all of the pictures in this book are either family photos (if she's in them) or author's own photography.

ISBN: 978-1-4759-7594-9 (sc)
ISBN: 978-1-4759-7595-6 (hc)
ISBN: 978-1-4759-7596-3 (e)

Library of Congress Control Number: 2013902856

Printed in the United States of America

iUniverse rev. date: 2/18/2013

My hope is that within these pages I enlighten you about an ailment that does not define me, entertain you with the humor that does, and teach you that the object of this game is not only to do your best on your best day, but also to do your best on your worst day.

I dedicate this work to my love, my fellow road-tripper, and my sweet husband, Paul Raymond Burton. He's known throughout this book as Caveman, Nurse Ratchet, the Bastard, and of course Paulie, a name I've been calling him for more than twenty years. He is anything but mediocre.

I would also like to thank those of you who, through the years, have encouraged me to save these stories and photographs for the unlikely dream of publishing my own book. I didn't see this coming, but you believed.

And one more: a special shout-out to my newest fan, Mark Parrish, who served as the fresh set of eyes my manuscript needed to help me be sure these stories could be understood by anyone not the least bit familiar with Julie-speak. And Mark, the honor is still mine.

Contents

To the VA Staff!

And now from the book

"A Day in the Life of Julie"

" Sealed Tight"

At 5:30 this morning I went out to warm up my car. It snowed six inches yesterday and it was nineteen degrees out.

I tromped through the powder in the driveway and tried to open the door. With a very loud curse word, I discovered that the car door was completely frozen shut. In haste, because I was freezing quickly in the wind, I went around and tried the other three doors. All of them were sealed tight.

This has never happened to me and I survived a blizzard in Massachusetts, but in the last storm it happened to my friend, so I knew it wasn't some urban myth used to strike fear into Those Who Live Where It Doesn't Snow.

After I waded back through the drift and into the warm house, I woke my husband up and asked what the trick was to get frozen car doors open.

He told me to pour water on them.

I asked, "Won't that just glaze them?" and before he drifted off to sleep again he mumbled, "Pour and pull."

So, I grabbed a pitcher and filled it with water thinking, "Pour and pull. Pour and pull."

Out through the snow to my frozen car I went.

Once there, I grabbed the handle and poured the water over the damned jammed door jamb and pulled.

Absolutely nothing happened. And now I had a freshly glazed car. It was quite pretty, actually. It glistened in the distant porch light.

I tried out some new curse words, prayed to some other gods and realized that I had splattered water down my front, so now I was glazed as well.

I tried some karate kicks (it's a plastic car) to the door hoping to break the seal, much like you would bang a jar on the countertop to break the vacuum. I tried pulling the handle with both hands and, in sheer frustration, I tried just staring stupidly at it as well. It wasn't budging.

So now I thought that I would have to call into work for a snow day. I didn't want to do that because I like going to work, and I like getting paid for going to work, but I figured my day was blown.

Maybe I could come out at the top of every hour and try again.

Then, a new idea dawned on me. I reached into my pocket and pulled out my keys. I thought this was a good idea: it might just work. I took a deep breath, closed my eyes and pushed a button on my keychain and – BAM! – *all four doors unlocked*.

Welcome to a day in the life of Julie.

"Tennis Toe"

Tennis season is upon us.

Last Wednesday was our first game. This is the fourth season for my friend Kristy and me, and the second for my husband. He's partnered with Taylor, Kristy's young daughter. Years ago, she could do little more than hit a ball against a fence off in the corner while her mom and I played, but now she's getting serious and is pretty good at returning the ball. Don't feel bad that she's playing with a bunch of adults: we all fear her on the court.

Last season ended with a sports injury. Paulie developed what could only be called *tennis toe*. The big toe nail-bed on his right foot turned black and unhappy from repeated quick stops and turns.

Midwinter I was horrified to watch him lift his nail up like a car hood and squeeze the last of the tube of Neosporin under it before dropping it back down and re-wrapping it safely up again.

After I realized I wasn't going to vomit after all, I shuddered, "Good lord man, how did you do that again?"

Now, this is a guy who never whines about pain, never cries about slamming his thumb in a double-paned sliding glass door, or removing the tip of his finger by one of those kitchen slicers when he ran the vegetable over the v-shaped blade (and didn't use the safety handle), or removing splinters from his hands after they've gone through his work gloves while working a twelve-hour shift at the mill years ago, but apparently he had reached his threshold with this injury because he barked, "*Tennis! Tennis damn it!* I hurt my toenail playing *tennis!*"

Unfortunately because of this fresh wound, the new season made him nervous and Kristy and I were getting pushback.

He said, "Just look at my toe. It's almost completely healed and now you want me to go out there and play on it again?"

"Yes."

"*Grrr,*" he growled.

Finally I said, "Clip your toe nails, take a Midol, *and let's go!*"

He was mystified, "Isn't that the one for cramps?"

I growled, "Yes, and crankiness. *Move it man!*"

The day and the hour finally arrived.

I dressed out at work and swung by the house to pick up The Man.

I put my hair up in ponytails so it wouldn't stick to my neck when I sweated (no worries there, it was 58 degrees on the court).

We stretched, warmed up and started in on the game. We don't use tennis scores, we play more like table tennis: first one to twenty-one wins. *Love* really does mean nothing to us.

Then the trash talk started and Kristy glared across the net at her 10-year-old daughter, "Do you want to get grounded?" My 38-year-old stopped mid-swing, dropped his racket and said in a small, worried voice, "No."

Kristy and I lost the season-opener.

"No worries," I said, "I don't care if we don't win the first one; I just want to be sure to win the season finale. Bragging rights for six-months, baby!!!"

Today, another Tennis Wednesday, was not so much a rain-check as a puddle-check. It rained all day so the courts were still wet after work. And it was 52 degrees.

Plenty of time to play. Plenty of time.

" 180 "

Things are still tough for us financially.

I was supposed to retire at forty as a self-made millionaire, but I just turned forty-one this month and after almost a decade of money, hopes, wishes and hard work, I've got nothing to show for my bright idea except for a patent. That's definitely something I'm proud of, but it's still just an expensive piece of paper.

So, things are tight. Paulie's got an excellent job. He's a nurse at a beautiful assisted living facility where the old ladies express their shock and dismay every time I cut his hair, "Oh no, where did all of your curls go?" and I'm in my fifth year at United Parcel Service, a place I am extremely happy to be at, but I would rather it be a place which I'd be extremely happy to retire from. Did that make sense? I rewrote that sentence four times, and the first time was probably the correct one but moving on…

Things are getting better, but very, very slowly. It's kind of like the economy… the country is happy that it found a twenty dollar bill in its purse, then, BAM, oil leaks all over the place fouling up beautiful coastline.

For us, though, it's not oil on the beaches, it's the car (this time, next month it'll be something else). The brakes let out a loud squeal when Paulie pulled into the carport.

He looked at me and said, "That should be taken care of."

I replied, "Way ahead of you, Skippy, the second quote I got was still above $300. So, how do the brakes sound now?"

"Perfect," spoketh the wise man.

Anyway, every once in a while, Paulie and I get depressed about our finances. When it gets real bad, we go to a place we call *La-La Land*. It's a very nice place to escape from reality. I don't think I'd stop volunteering or donating money in *La-La Land*, it is just a post-lottery or post-patent-gets-licensed-for-millions-of-dollars place where we can buy whatever we want without stressing about paying it off, or going without one thing in order to buy something that we needed even more, like a set of four new tires for the aforementioned car.

All of the things we buy in *La-La Land* are so special to us, that they get names.

I named his sail boat *Tails of the Wind*, my houseboat *Away From Home*, and my Friesian mare *Wild Mountain Honey*.

I would let him name his horse, but unfortunately he would call it *Buck*. It would have nothing to do with it being of the equine species though; he's wanted to name one of his pets Buck forever. What a complete lack of imagination: Buck. Ewww. Oh, please don't get me started. I have held off this wish of his for so long, that I am now quite exhausted. I'm so against this that I won't even let him name an *imaginary* pet Buck. Maybe I should get him a hamster and let him use up the name so when we get around to owning beautiful horses one of them won't be saddled with that unfortunate moniker.

Anyway, the other morning I moped around getting ready for work and ended up drifting off into *La-La Land*.

After brushing my teeth I jumped in the shower thinking what I was going to name our RV.

It would be a little motor home. Not tiny, but a place we can play cribbage or wrestle without breaking furniture. Again. And I do mean wrestle. A friend mistakenly thought it was a euphemism for sex.

Given our current weight class, you should be thinking Sumo rather than Greco-Roman wrestling, with an occasional WWF maneuver as I get one off the top rope screaming my rebel yell on the way down.

The most he usually has time for, when I do this leaping-from-the-rope, is to duck and cover. It looks kind of like the earthquake drills I had in elementary school in southern California: curl up into a ball, close your eyes tight, beware of breaking glass and don't come out until you hear the all-clear.

He's so adorable when I land on him after he forgot to curl up. That doesn't seem to happen very much anymore though.

Gosh, where was I?

Ok, naming the motorhome: I thought I would call it *Jack*, as in

(Let's) *Hit the Road Jack*. Ray Charles wrote a few songs about being "Busted", but this one does it for me.

Hit the road bad debt. Hit the road bad feelings. Hit the road bad weather. Hit the road bad day.

Then, unbeknownst to me, I started singing that song.

I didn't realize it until I saw my fifteen-year-old kitty cat who was sunning herself under the heat lamp on top of the fuzzy toilet seat cover suddenly sit up.

I grabbed the shampoo bottle and bellowed *"Whatchu say?!?"* and by the time I looked back down at her through the shower door she was gone.

But I kept singing, "…"

And that's how I did the 180 on my mood about money.

Whatchu say???

"Holiday Music & Leftovers"

Last night I was trying to wake Paulie up to watch Monday Night Football with me. He was burrowed under the covers with the cats on the bed and he just wouldn't get up. I'm tugging and pulling and landing on him (cats are gone by now), but he refused to budge.

He kept mumbling about how warm and cozy it was under the covers, so I offered him, uh, *marital relations* instead of getting out of bed to go downstairs to watch MNF.

He said no.

"Are you *insane*? Do you have *any idea* how many men would love to be offered the choice of *football* or *relations* from their wives, and you have the gall to turn them *both* down?!? Oh, no way! *That does it mister!*"

So, I put in a Christmas CD. I didn't even have to turn up the volume before the man launched himself out of the covers. It worked faster than opening the blinds and turning all of the lights on. Just as soon as Rosemary Clooney started warbling about the happy holidays, he felt much worse, and I felt much better.

All was right in the world.

Three weeks later…

A few minutes after Paulie went up to bed, I went into the bedroom and made sure the blinds were closed tight because he can't sleep when it's light out (he works nights), turned the fan on because he can't sleep hot, and kicked on the CD player because he needs a bit of music to drift off, and then I went back downstairs.

Hours later he came downstairs, sat on the couch to put his shoes on and then stopped and glared up at me.

"Ok," he said, "What the hell did I do wrong now?"

Apparently, there was still a Christmas CD in our five-CD

stereo, and that's what I accidentally clicked on right before I left the room.

I thought I was playing Pink Floyd.

I seriously doubt he got any sleep because he was, most likely, scrolling through his actions of the last week or so, trying to figure out what he'd done that was so bad that I had to play Christmas music when he was trying to get to sleep for work.

"Oh, no! I am so sorry! Where, by the way, is that disc now?"

He gruffed, "It's probably lodged in the wall on the far side of the bedroom."

Note to self: Be sure to remove *all* holiday music from players after the season is over.

" Wishboned "

Paulie and I argue a lot, but not like most couples (no surprise there, right?).

Mostly it's "No, you take the last cookie" type of stuff that has made at least one friend say, "Jeez, you two are disgusting."

We seem to be a jolly pair looking out for each other and sharing the best in life with each other, but that's not how it always goes, because we are fairly certain that we would fight to the proverbial death over a pair of binoculars.

After a struggle that took us to the floor, we would both come up and start dancing around winded and gleeful in our victory over the other, only to discover that we each were the proud new owner of a monocular.

Scientifically, it would probably be as exactly split as a wishbone we snapped a few years ago that, to our utter amazement, was exactly (probably molecularly) divided down the middle of the damn thing. We absolutely *could not* determine a winner. It was divided exactly in half like cellular mitosis.

So, as good as we are to each other, we can't seem to share everything.

Incidentally, don't loan us your binoculars.

"My Hero"

PAULIE

Paulie came home from work this morning and told me that a resident unexpectedly died last night.

The frantic caregiver for that floor called him (he's a nurse in an assisted living facility) up to the room and he discovered the resident face down on the floor. When he rolled him over he saw that the resident had already passed, but he proceeded to give CPR and ordered the caregiver to call 911 immediately.

Either the caregiver was too rattled to explain the situation, or her accent was too strong under these circumstances, but she ended up having to hand the phone off to Paulie.

During chest compressions he yelled into the phone, "85-year-old male, non-responsive, no heartbeat or breathing and he is cyanotic."

The 911 operator asked if he needed to be guided through how to do CPR and he said he was already doing it. Then he threw the phone up on the bed and told the still-unglued caregiver to go find help.

When others showed up he pointed and said, "You, go outside and wait for the ambulance and make sure they can get in through the doors. You, go sit with his wife and just tell her he's collapsed, nothing more."

He continued attempting cardiopulmonary resuscitation until emergency services arrived and unpacked. He finally stepped back when they took over and, for another thirty minutes, tried to revive him. They, too, were unsuccessful.

While they were in the room working on him, Paulie went to get the resident's medication list for the medics, and then visited the wife of 57 years who lived there too (she has Parkinson's), and told her that it didn't look like her husband would make it, so she needed to prepare herself for the worst.

Through his years as a nurse Paulie's pronounced about a dozen people dead, but they were all because they didn't wake up in the morning.

He said that this was the first time he'd ever given CPR to a real person.

It was all unexpected (it's believed the resident had a massive heart attack and died within minutes), and Paulie believed he handled it well.

Then my hero said, "You know, the funny thing is I forgot to spit my gum out. I just automatically parked it behind my lip seconds before I started giving him mouth-to-mouth."

Jokingly, I replied, "You had it when you were done though, right?"

"Yeah."

Seriously, I asked, "And it's not the same piece you're chewing now, right?"

"No."

"Oh, Paulie! You did such a good job. I'm so proud of you! Now, go wash your face and brush your teeth and use plenty of mouth wash, and then come give me kisses."

My hero.

"Perfect Wife"

Yesterday, Paulie discovered that his new (old) car is a rusted out piece of junk that could fall apart at any time. The engine light came on the day after he brought it home, so Paulie took it in to a local place (he bought the car in Seattle) to see what might be wrong.

The mechanic was going to unscrew something to look at the front-end drive and decided not to because he was afraid he would be unable to put it all back together again because of the massive corrosion.

Paulie didn't have it checked by a mechanic before he bought it because he was pressed for time. He also didn't have many choices because he couldn't spend a lot of money. The salesman knew this.

The car hasn't fallen apart yet, so he'll just use it as a to-and-from work car and mine for everything else. It's a very tough blow for him.

He said he almost bought a bottle on the way home.

Now, my first husband was an AA-type of alcoholic. We didn't keep alcohol in the house and one slip would send him into a huge turmoil (he only slipped once in the years that I knew him). He always carried his Alcoholics Anonymous chip in his pocket and his sponsor was his best man at our wedding.

Paulie is different. We get silly with shots or drink microbrews on sandwich night. I've got an aging bottle of rum in the freezer and an equally old bottle of Patron Silver on the countertop (it'll probably evaporate through the cork before I finish it off). He's got Kokanee beer in the fridge and Jameson in the freezer. On very rare occasions, we belly up to the bar and run up a tab or have three margaritas with a two hour dinner.

Paulie used to drink a lot and, through the years, I've asked him to go for quality not quantity. But, when things get rough, he reverts to behaviors he learned in childhood to deal with the beatings and the verbal abuse and escapes to the safe place of an alcoholic stupor.

Hourly, daily, weekly, monthly, he's fine with alcohol, but when Kelsey's birthday or the anniversary of his grandfather's death used to roll around I'd come home to find him literally and figuratively bottled-up.

I've asked that he face those painful feelings and work through them rather than cut and run, and he's done amazingly well without the soft, padded daze of inducement.

This time, when he got upset about the damned car, I asked him not to cascade into a total crash and burn. Depression with me (now) starts with one bummer, and then I think of another, then another, then another until I'm just royally upset. Once there, I have a hell of a time getting out of it. It used to be immeasurably worse, but this, mercifully, is where I am now.

He said he already crashed and burned, but instead of drinking into it he came home and slept through it and now he's feeling somewhat better, but still bummed.

I said, "Congratulations! Thank you for not getting a bottle. Thank you thank you thank you!"

Then somewhere, in that same conversation, I heard, "Perfect wife."

One of us said it, but I've had a cold for the past week so I'm all stuffed up and kind of out of it, so I wasn't sure just *who* said it.

"Whoa, whoa, whoa. Stop! Did you just say I'm a perfect wife?"

He looked right at me and said yes.

I quickly inquired, "Are you sure you wouldn't want something tucked, sucked, or lifted on me? Or, do you want me to do something or not do something? Am I too loud? Am I not nice enough? Am I too opinionated? Do you want me to dress more feminine?" I'd rather wear flannel, jeans and hiking boots and go tromping through the forest with my hair tucked back in a ponytail than wear ruffles, bows and a skirt with high heel shoes, headed for the mall.

He said no.

"Isn't there anything you'd like me to work on? Is there anything that you don't like or is there something that drives you nuts and you desperately want me to stop doing?"

He, again, said no.

"Oh, wow. Thank you so much, my love. That's amazing."

Then I started looking for pen and paper and said, "Well, come sit down next to me and I'll just jot down some things I want you to change immed…"

I looked up and he was gone.

Fortunately, the man has a sense of humor.

As it says in our wedding vows, "You may not be a perfect man, but you're the perfect man for me."

At "Pool & Pizza," Pearl Harbor, Hawaii, 1993

"Once Upon A Time"

Once upon a time, I was lonely and depressed.

I was unhappy in almost every way I can imagine.

I lived in Texas, in what was actually a nice apartment, getting a wonderful education because they have the best colleges, but I was done with living in the desert. Although both of my bloodlines go through the state (Phillips/Odom/Chisholm and McCulloch/Smith/Scott/Adams), I wasn't from there and never felt at home... that location just felt wrong to me.

Everything just felt upset, mixed up, fractured and backwards.

Then, ten years ago tomorrow, Christmas Day, the man I had always loved came down from his heaven (Washington, his home state) and proposed to me in my hell (Texas).

He scooped me up into his arms with an important question on his mind and I said, "Yes, you bastard, what took you so long?" We kissed, and all was soon to be right with the world.

We threw all my belongings into the back of a rented moving van and drove all the way up to heaven (as it turns out, there's no actual stairway, it's really a road).

We arrived on December 31, 2000, right in time for the brand new year.

We married and had a year or two of bliss before things went terribly wrong and he divorced me shortly after our third uncelebrated, painful, anniversary.

I survived remarkably well, but he sent himself down into his own hell.

Two years later, we found each other again, I asked him to marry me, he said yes, and the bliss was far better than we'd ever known.

Far better than our first marriage.

Far better than any other relationship than we had had with any other person on the planet.

Far better… it is just far better.

As this ten-year anniversary is upon us, I find that we are both in a very good place.

And, after I remind him of this very special anniversary, and he replies, "Oh, huh. Really? Well that's cool," we'll hug and kiss and gather up our gifts and go to the family house to celebrate with food, friends and loved ones, just as it should be.

We are both happy and healthy, which is all I've ever wished.

Things are changing, of course.

I discovered, while crocheting him an afghan, that I now need bifocals for the close work. Presbyopia: What an "Oh, crap" feeling.

Money is still incredibly tight. I'm getting my finances out of the hole from this recession and a past surgery, but his is still reeling from bad decisions of yester-year. For someone so smart, decent, kind and loving, he really trips up on some important life choices. Two weeks ago in front of his brother and uncle he said to me, "Ok, from now on, you are going to make all of my financial decisions for me." Just what every wife wants to hear.

We are feeling a bit tight in our apartment. It has two stories, for crying out loud, but it's still jammed between two other apartments. He spent six years in the barracks and on a submarine, and I spent eight years in boarding school dorm rooms and the barracks in the Navy: we're just ready to be more alone in the world and not so claustrophobically challenged.

Speaking of which, in an attempt at peace on earth and good will towards others, I bought Oreos for our next-door neighbor. I was going to present them to her and her two teenagers and ask them to kindly stop letting their front door slam. It's horrendous and shakes our entire home and my man is a day-sleeper, so he hears and feels most of it.

When Paulie discovered what I was about to do, he softly whispered, "Oh, hell no!!!"

He said, "You can do whatever you want" (*duh*), "but I vote that we do not give them double-stuffed Oreos because they always let their damn front door slam."

I insisted, "That's exactly why I want to give it to them. It'd be kind of a peace offering before I make my request."

He, again, said no.

So, we poured two glasses of milk and ripped into the package ourselves. Man, those are the best freakin' Oreos I have ever tasted in my entire life. Ever. What made them all the better you ask? The white Christmas peace-offering bow was still stuck to the top of the package.

This year we did not feel we could spend the money on a tree, so as with recent previous years, we got a wreath instead.

We are very content.

Our little family was never able to produce children, but he has me and I have him and we have made a home.

Zander & Zoe.

In our home we have twin girls Zoe ("the Quiet One") and Zander ("Cupcake"). Zoe's the gray and white short-haired peaceful one, while her sister's black and white long-hair goofy one. Even as adults, they sleep together like this.

ECHO.

We also have Echo (lovingly called "the Fat Hobbit"). She is perpetually glued to Paulie, although here she'd pushed my laptop aside to take over. Oddly, if I whistle to her, she will meow back. Whistle*Meow. Whistle*Meow. Whistle*Meow. She *literally* echoes me. I didn't know she would do this when I named her years ago, and she doesn't do this with anyone else.

OCTOBER FEST.

And then there's my beloved October Fest ("Toby"), who just turned sixteen. She's older than all of our other cats *combined*. We love her deeply, and she returns the love ten-fold.

<small>BUCK THE GUINEA PIG.</small>

Newest to our abode, is a beloved, black and white smooth-haired Guinea pig that goes by the name of Buck.

You may think this is too may animals, but we'd actually have more if we had property. Some people have four kids or four dogs: we have four cats and piglet. It's a good start.

So, when we all wrap up this year with peace, love and joy (except for our door-slamming-Oreo-deprived-noisy-neighbors), and Paulie holds me tight and showers kisses on me this New Year's Eve, I'll feel safe, warm, loved and hug him tightly back, and at midnight-oh-one I'll look up into his kind, gentle, quiet eyes and say to him, "Someday, my prince will come."

"Names & Faces"

I went by the florist at the local grocery store I love so much to hunt for another plant for my desk at work.

Settling on a jade after going over several other species with the woman there, I asked what her name was.

When she told me, I said, "Hi, my name is Julie."

Now, as Paulie would tell you, I introduce myself to everyone and I remember their names very well (remarkable for the occasionally Swiss-cheesed brain of mine).

I introduce myself to the maid at a motel we're staying in for one night, the waiters, the guy who does repairs at our apartment complex, the guy who empties trash at work, the cab drivers, receptionists, mail carriers, grocery checkouts... on and on.

Eye contact, a hello, I call them by their name if they have a tag, and if time, a name exchange and handshake.

Once, after my car was serviced, a guy brought it around to the front, got out, took off his clean gloves and held the door open for me.

I said, "Thank you, very much," and offered him my hand.

He waved me off and said, "My hands are filthy."

I looked him in the eye and replied, "That's ok," and we shook. A look changed in his eyes. It was wonderful.

But, even with all of this socializing, it freaks me out when people remember *me*.

I don't feel that visible or memorable to human beings. I often feel small and stupid. Unimportant. Unremarkable. Mediocre.

Back to the florist, who was boxing up my little jade plant...

She stopped suddenly, turned to me and said, "*That's* how I remember you!"

"Um. What? How do you remember me?"

"I also work in the bakery."

A little tickle started in my tummy, and I cracked a smile. She made my wedding cake four years ago for when I remarried Paulie.

"And what did the cake have on it, may I ask???"

She said, "A beach scene because you met in Hawaii, and the word "bastard" on it. It said, "Julie & the Bastard". I have never *in my life* made a wedding cake with the word "bastard" on it."

On March 3, 2008, I remarried Paulie.

She breathed a sigh of relief when I told her we were still together, and actually celebrating this month the 20-year anniversary of our first date. She probably thought she'd jinxed the whole marriage with that silly cake.

And then she giggled.

I don't think she will ever forget me.

"Nurse Ratchet Dispenses Advice"

On Tuesday afternoon, I vomited at work.

On Wednesday, I stayed home from work.

This morning, I scrapped myself out of bed, showered, clothed myself, and went downstairs sweltering.

Paulie was eating his dinner, because he'd just come home from his night shift as a nurse. He was eating cheap canned chili with hot, melted cheese floating in the grease on top. A new wave of nausea hit me at the sight and smell of it.

I was holding my elbows out as I fanned myself and plucked at my shirt. Normally chilled to the bone, I asked him, "Is it hot in here?"

Normally broiling in fifty-degree weather, he replied, "No. Actually, it's not hot at all."

"I'm sweating and feel over-heated. I opened all of the windows upstairs, and I just feel terrible."

Nurse Ratchet began his series of questions but then suddenly stopped right after he felt my forehead.

"Do you have a fever?"

"I don't know."

"Come here: let me feel your forehead."

Uncomfortably eyeballing his disgusting dinner, I moved in within range so he could assess the damage and advise the best care in the most kind and loving way. Kind and loving. Kind and loving. Awww, my man is going to take care of me...

"You are freezing and sweaty."

"What does that mean?"

"It means," he got up to wash his hands, "*stay away from me.*"

"Every Sailor's Got Their Own Story of How They Got Crabs"

Paulie and I went to Joe's Crab Shack, a favorite of ours when we go visit my parents. We feasted on seafood, drank margaritas, and before we left, we bought about six different tee-shirts, and one of them said, "got crabs?"

Paulie is particularly proud of the time he got crabs in the Navy, and yes, I have my own story too, which I will relate here as well...

PAULIE & ME AT JOE'S CRAB SHACK, GRAPEVINE TEXAS, 2011.

Paulie went to an overnight-tents-around-the-campfire beerfest on one of the beaches at Bellows Air Force Base on Oahu, with his shipmates and their friends. Everyone drank until they could no longer stand up straight. Standard fair for a bunch of submariners, their barracks parties were legendary.

Eventually, the fire died down and the beer ran out, so these protectors of the American way of life went to sleep it off in the tents.

Hours later, Paulie woke up alone on a deserted beach.

Still drunk, he lifted himself up off the wet sand and discovered that, in fact, he was not alone.

He was covered in crabs. Fiddler crabs. Whenever he tells this story (usually with my urging), I picture the scene from *Jaws* when Crissy Watkins's remains were found on the beach the next morning with crabs crawling all over her.

He said he was so freaked that he vomited the whole way back to the campsite.

Did he learn from this? Are you kidding? Bellows Air Force Base was always good for overnight camping and he wasn't about to give that up. Sheesh, people...

My story's a little bit different.

My best friend in the Navy, Muriel (Moe) Amadoro, and I were in a meeting in a large conference room with a bunch of people. We were only E-4s, and where we worked (four-star admiral commanding), we were pretty low on the totem pole.

Moe & Me drinking in Waikiki, 1993

I can't remember who was in the meeting, but I think our lieutenant was the highest ranking one there. I do know that of the dozen or so personnel, we were the only females – embarrassing, when you read the end of my story.

I can't remember what the meeting was about, but it droned on and on.

It went on for so long that eventually I tuned it out and, unfortunately, started focusing on my own severe discomfort.

Finally, not being able to stand it anymore, I leaned over and whispered something into Moe's ear.

She gasped, her body went rigid, and she said - loudly - "No I don't have anything for crabs! That's disgusting! Get away from me!"

The speaker stopped speaking and everyone in the room turned to stare.

Before Muriel's chair stopped rolling away from me, I said to her - and the room - "I said *cramps*. Do you have anything for *cramps*?"

Honestly, I don't remember anything that happened after that.

"Spontaneity"

I broiled Italian sausages and pork chops in a shallow pan after dumping a whole bottle of marinade over them. When they were almost done, I cut up an onion and threw it in there too. Paulie was completely ecstatic with just the smell emanating from the kitchen and could barely wait for it to come out of the oven. My carnivorous caveman has no patience. Next time, I guess, I'll cut it all up and throw it in the crock pot.

That same day, I crocheted a hat on a whim with no pattern to follow. It's a double-strand (dark brown and soft brown) so it's thick and warm, and it has quite a few goofy braids coming out of the top as a final flourish.

I put it on my head while I was crocheting a matching scarf, also *sans* pattern.

When Paulie came downstairs from his nap, he kept staring at my head. That unnerved me, and I began to think that the hat was really ugly.

I asked him why he thought about it and he said it was really nice. I said, "Thank you! I crocheted it while you were sleeping."

"Really? I was trying to figure out where you might have *bought* it."

He wore it in sub-zero temperatures, and now he wants one too.

People at work really like the matching set (hat and scarf), and it was suggested that I make some to donate to the United Way when we have our next silent auction.

How cool is that???

"Whipped & Creamed"

Last year, about this time when it was getting cold like this, I huddled in the easy chair with a blanket when Paulie got up from the couch to open the sliding glass door for one of the cats that was glaring at him. Then he left it opened and turned to go back to the couch.

I said, "Please close that, I'm feeling cold."

"But the cats want to go out."

"I know," I replied, "but it's cold out and I'm already chilled. And, anyway," I said jokingly, "I outrank the cats." (ha ha ha)

He turned back to the slider, touched it and stopped.

"I do outrank the cats, don't I?"

Silence.

"Hey!"

He jumped, "What?"

"I outrank the cats in this house, right?"

"Uh…"

"HEY!!!"

Nothing.

"You're a caveman, and they have fur coats, but I am cold. Close the door, or I'm going to turn the heat on."

That did it. *That's* what it took.

He grumbled because for the rest of the night (and season) he knew he'd be getting up to let the cats in, up to let the cats out, up to let the cats in, up to let the cats out…

I grumbled because I almost lost out to the damn pets!

Even Buck the Guinea Pig has him wrapped around his paw. Paulie will walk by and Buck will sound off for more food. "I just fed you an hour ago! Look! You're standing on it!" All Buck has to do is one more squeak and Paulie's off to the fridge to get him a carrot.

It just dawned on me why he has me look after the fish tank and plants: they don't have him whipped, so he has no use for them in his life.

Wow, that was a close call with the cats though.

Way too close.

"Give Me What I Want and I'll Go Away"

The other day I ran around the coffee table to Paulie who was lying flat out on the couch watching football.

As I leaped into the air forming a perfect swan dive, he started screaming, and then I flattened out for the most spectacular belly flop landing ever. On him.

"Give me what I want and I'll go away," I said.

"No! No, no, no, no. *No! You don't always go away.* I'm not falling for that again."

Still lying on him, "Ok, I'll just hang out here then. Oh, what was that sound? Was that your back snapping? Must be what an avalanche sounds like right before it lets go."

Seconds pass…

"Oh, God. Ok. What do you want?!?"

Apparently, I can be very annoying.

But we knew that already, didn't we?

"Floor to Ceiling"

Yesterday, when Paulie and I met in the hallway (he was coming home from work, I was about to head out), I harassed him about his clothes.

"Aw, did your mommy-in-law dress you today?"

He was clothed in a shirt, pants and socks that Mom bought him on our trip down to see them in August. He looked spiffy and comfy instead of threadbare and worn out.

Looking down at himself, and embarrassed, "Uh. No. She…she *bought* them. I can still dress myself, you know."

As he walked away, the harassment continued, "Aw, she wuves her Paulie."

From floor to ceiling, wrapped in his mother-in-law's love.
Awww.

PS – His mother-in-law loves this story.

"Not Death & Taxes"

A co-worker had to leave early today, and on her way out the door she said that she had to go get two very unpleasant things done this afternoon.

Someone from the back row piped up, "A mammogram?!?"

She blushed and said, "Oh, no! I'm going to the dentist then to an appointment to get my taxes done."

"Smoke Signals"

I've never stayed very long with someone who, if I continued the relationship, would turn me into a nag.

I don't like having to remind an adult to clean up after himself, help with dinner, or smaller but more important stuff like call me if you're going to be late. It's not worth it to me.

In a solid relationship, I like open conversation and suggestions both ways. I listen, and if I don't like the suggestion I will tell him. He has the same option.

To keep from becoming an angry person about trivial things, I've thought of clever, honest, fair-warning ways to speak with my mate…

When his week of doing dishes was over, and it was my turn, I'd usually start out by unloading the dishwasher that he filled up and ran. When I tried to put clean dishes away, I'd find things like food stuck to the silverware.

In our new apartment, the dishwasher was different, so I'd have to say, "Hey, these aren't getting clean like they used to. You have to scrub the food off; all the dishwasher does is sanitize."

When my week rolled around again, and it happened again, I said, "Look at these, sweetie. You can actually do this however you want, but these aren't getting clean. I'll take over the kitchen when it's clean." It was sound and reasonable so he did it, and then I did it. We've never had to speak of it again.

Another odd thing he used to do when it was his turn to change the bed, was to sweep up the bed skirt and shove it under the mattress with the fitted sheet. Our newly made bed looked like a woman who'd gotten her dress caught in her pantyhose after using the bathroom. I thought it looked obvious, but he didn't see it. I said, "You're so cute. Watch this." Then I untucked it. We didn't fight about it. It never happened again. No big deal.

It would be a big deal if he (or I) refused to listen and got angry, but we've learned that flying off the handle and shouting about something stupid just isn't worth the anguish of a fight. He's got his quirks that I try to honor, too.

Ok, one more for you. This is more along the lines of "How to piss off a caveman," but I don't ever have to grumble about this again...

He's got beautiful feet, and I love his toes dearly, but for a brief time in our relationship, his toenails were ragged and long.

I said, "Please cut your toenails," one too many times before I finally said, "If you don't cut your toenails, I'm going to paint them bright red when you are sleeping."

He must have thought I was joking.

I wasn't.

Wow, he was *not* a happy camper, but we never fight about this now because he keeps his toenails trimmed.

It must sound like I'm a tyrannical woman and wife, but I'm not. This is a safe, happy, warm home filled with love. And compromise. And bartering. And trade-offs. It works for us, others do it another way.

"My" way can't be too foreign to him though, because he told me this story about the part of his family tree that probably doesn't branch out very much: the Stones.

Mr. and Mrs. Stone were fighting for days, maybe even weeks, about how she wanted to move closer to town, but he said no.

Every time, he said no.

One morning, they fought about it, he gave the same answer, and he then stormed off.

In the evening, when he returned home he saw his wife sitting in the front yard.

In her chair.

All of the inside furniture was, in fact, now outside.

And behind that, he could see that the house was mostly through the process of being burned to the ground.

My guess is they moved closer to town not too long after the smoke cleared.

When Paulie first told me that story, though, he was truly incredulous, but I was thinking; "Now that's not a bad idea..."

"A Mouth-Breathing, Knuckle-Dragging, Sick Troll"

I was sick for a week with a cold, thankful it wasn't the flu.

When I got better, Paulie got sick.

For a while he just kept insisting that it was just his sinuses. I knew it wasn't and tried to dote on him because he's always so good to me when I'm sick, but he repeatedly rejected my kindness.

"Would you like more water?"

"No."

"Tissue?"

"No."

"Toast?"

"No."

"Soup?"

"No."

"Would you like me to leave you alone?"

"N-*Yes!*"

"Ah, trick question!"

Then I landed on him for kisses and he bellowed.

Eventually, he went to work. On the way out the door, he was still insisting it was just his sinuses but came home after a twelve-hour shift, a mouth-breathing, knuckle-dragging, drooling, exhausted troll.

"Not just sinuses, is it?"

Awww.

Listen to that.

Another bellow.

"Caveman No Read Books"

Caveman no read books.

He's a unique one, though.

He's extremely smart and can tear apart a textbook to ace a course, but he doesn't really read for pleasure.

He reads a book every four years.

Not four books a year: a book every four years.

Not a book for six months, then no book for the next three and a half years.

The same book takes four years to read.

In contrast, I am a voracious reader. I always have four or five books on my nightstand that I have going at the same time, plus one at work.

Last night I told Paulie that I had just finished another book. He was as excited as if I had said, "In one more minute, it'll be 8:33PM."

He got even less interested in sticking around when I started talking about it.

"It's called *The Universe in a Nutshell* and it's by Stephen Hawking. Another book I've read of his was *A Brief History of Time*. I really enjoyed them and will have to go back to the bookstore and look for more."

When I looked up at him, his eyes had lost their focus and glazed over.

"And last night, I finished Khaled Hosseini's *A Thousand Splendid Suns*, a story taking place in Afghanistan. The other book he wrote is called *The Kite Runner* which I haven't read yet. Come on," I said, reaching out, "touch it. Touch the book."

"No."

"I know you want to."

"No."

"Come on. I see you checking out my bookshelves when you think I'm not looking. Just touch it."

"No. And you can't make me."

It was the dumbest thing I've ever heard him say: I threw the book at him.

He recoiled and screamed as I would have if someone had tossed me a handful of rosy-kneed tarantula.

The paperback hit him and fell to the floor.

"You touched it."

That did it. He grunted, turned around and left the room.

I didn't see him again until this morning.

" *BAM* "

Last weekend we had assumed our usual football positions: I was in the easy chair and he was laid out on the couch.

Exciting games, really.

Right before my Patriots won the game and were on their way to their fifth Super Bowl since 2001, I was out of the chair, screaming and jumping up and down.

As I rounded the coffee table and launched myself into the air, I hear Paulie, far below me, *scream*.

"Aw," I thought, "Isn't that sweet? He's happy New England is going to the Super Bowl too! Oh, how I do love him!"

Then, as I finish the apex of my jump, and begin to fall back to Earth and into my man's arms, I hear this, "I'm afraid I am actually suffering right now with *quite a bit* of back pain. Is there any way you can wave off your landing?"

"Oh, honey. No. I'll be there in just a few sec..."

BAM

I heard something crunch that sounded like one of those aluminum can compactors that recyclers use. I think I hurt his back.

Or bent his knee backwards.

Or something.

I don't know, I wasn't really paying attention because...

My Patriots are going to the Super Bowl!!!

Woo hoo!!!

"Carte Blanche Reading"

Years ago, when we were both struggling like hell because of the economy and our own personal money problems, I told Paulie that my La-La Land dream was to have enough money to walk into Barnes & Noble for a *carte blanche* shopping spree.

He was quiet, so I wasn't sure he heard me.

When I looked at him, he had turned a sickly green and looked rather disgusted.

I quickly clarified my statement, "I would read every single last book I bought. Most of them I would even read twice."

He choked back on the bile rising in his gorge and said that that's what scared him the most.

"Score One for the Wife"

The man and I were watching a movie here at home last weekend. He was sprawled on the couch and I was, once again, in the easy chair.

He had a big bowl of popcorn and I was nibbling at a few foil-covered chocolate Easter eggs.

Somewhere near the end of his bowl, I flicked in the foil wrappers and scored two points without him even noticing.

Two bites and one foil-to-filling later he was on his feet, spitting it out and hissing and cursing my name.

Score one for the wife.

"Boxers or Briefs?"

I was twirling around in the bedroom this morning in my new bra and underwear before I got dressed to go to work and after Paulie came home from work.

When I noticed him standing in the doorway watching me, I twirled again and said, "Look! Look! I've got new underclothes! I know they don't match like my old stuff did, but they don't have any holes in them where they're not supposed to and the elastic's not shot. Aren't they awesome?"

I have miraculously paid off my bills and gotten rid of the horrid credit cards and am now, finally, buying much needed clothes.

I needed work shoes, and got two pair, also underwear, bras, work socks and work pants.

Paulie wasn't too impressed because a) he's still deeply in debt and b) my mother bought him work pants, work shirts, and work socks when we visited last August. I was so grateful to her for that because I couldn't take care of him myself and he most definitely couldn't do it either.

After another few twirls, jazz hands, and a giddy "Ta da!" I looked up only to see him turn and walk away.

Then I heard…

"We need to go back to Texas. I need new boxers."

" Building a Rabbit Hutch"

Spring is here so I came up with the obligatory Honey-Do list for Paulie. Before I presented it to him last night, I gave a short preamble.

"I know it's a long list, but these are important to me, and I hope you can get them done by the end of summer. It would make me very happy."

When I handed the sheet of paper over to him, he tried to poker-face it, but I saw him heave a huge sigh of relief.

It was a list of places I'd like to go walking with him: Sunset Pond, Mt Baker, Deception Pass, Silver Lake, Mile Marker 38 on Mt Baker Highway, Lakes Padden and Samish, Highway 20, the waterfront, downtown, Fairhaven, La Conner, Winthrop, Leavenworth…

His initial apprehension was a conditioned response to my usually loaded questions.

One time I came home on a Friday afternoon and asked him what he was doing that weekend.

He rattled off some things and I said, "Nope."

"Ok, so what am I doing then?"

"Building a rabbit hutch."

"We don't even *have* a rabb… Oh, crap."

" Over the River "

One of my coworkers is out for a week because she went with her husband to Kentucky to see his family.

I was thinking about how our weather here has been sixty degrees and rainy, when someone spoke up and asked, "I wonder what the weather's like in Kentucky now, but I've never been."

It went from desk to desk, "Me neither," "Me neither."

When it got to me, I said, "I've been there."

They all perked up and one inquired, "What's the weather like there?"

I replied, "Ohio."

Apparently, no one's been there either.

"Dinner & Dessert"

I made a new recipe of chocolate chip oatmeal cookies. I had three dozen cooling on waxed paper for a very brief moment in time.

Then I made two slabs of dry rubbed, roasted and then crock-potted barbeque baby-back ribs.

Paulie came downstairs growling that he couldn't sleep through the smell of my cooking. He'd been salivating for hours before he gave up trying.

I wanted to share both the cookies and the ribs with the family, maybe take over a care package or something, but Paulie started bargaining with me. Some of the cookies made it out of the house; the ribs didn't have a chance.

Days later…

The cookies and ribs are gone.

I smuggled out some cookies for people at work and they loved them.

One person said, "Oh my god, they taste like Costco cookies!"

"Hey, these are homemade!"

She quickly said, "I know, I know! Calm down, Julie! That was a compliment."

Paulie was grumbling again about the ribs, but this time it was that he had to stop eating them so he could go to sleep. He said he fought getting a "second dose," but knew he couldn't stuff himself and sleep well after.

(Insert evil laugh here).

"I Win!"

Paulie and I rarely fight. I'd say it's a once-a-year type of thing.

We'd rather tease, harass, laugh, say "You're right," make bets, knuckle under, wrestle, debate, hope the other person's in a good mood when you're feeling yucky, and, if all else fails, compromise.

And we talk about everything.

A while ago, death was the subject.

I told him that I could still see my sixteen-year-old self at my precious father's grave thinking that he was moldering under my feet. It was a powerful emotion that was all mixed in with the dreadful grief. I had, right then and there, made the decision to be cremated after death. I even cremate our kitty cats after they die. I feel strongly about this.

Then Paulie told me his final wishes.

I don't remember what they were, I wasn't really paying attention, but somewhere near the end of his soliloquy, I interrupted and said, "If you wish for a coffin, and you die first, I will honor that."

"But just know that I'll bury you in a suit and tie." (gasp)

"And I'll make sure that it's all 100% polyester so that in a bazillion years, when H. G. Wells' morlocks dig you up, that suit and tie will still be there." (groan)

"And, at your wake, I'll put in my Barry Manilow CD, play it loud, and insist that it was yours."

I win!

" Bonfire "

April 29, 2007.

Two years after he divorced me, Paulie and I started dating again.

I moved back in with him just four months ago.

Last night, Paulie started a bonfire. I went out and joined him after dark, and we sat out there until the wee hours of the morning. We enjoy each other's company and spoke of many things.

He was clearly depressed with so much on his mind, but something in particular was bothering him, and it took a while for him to say what it was.

Eventually has asked if I was ready to talk about Holly, my nine-year-old cat that I had to put down five months ago. I took it really poorly and couldn't yet talk about her death. Now, he felt, it was time.

She had cancer.

I discovered lumps on her leg and ribcage, figured out what it was, and cried all night because I knew her end was near.

The next morning, I called the vet, my friend Kristy, and Paulie, who'd just come home from his two jobs and was about to go to sleep.

They both met me at the clinic, the doctor gave his diagnosis, which agreed with my presumption, and then Paulie stayed in the room with Holly while I left the room, crying my eyes out.

I looked at Paulie in the light of the bonfire and saw tears rolling down his face, but that day in the vet's office there weren't any. I thought he'd slipped into his "nurse mode" and stayed with Holly while she slipped away because he felt comfortable with it.

Actually, it hurt him badly. He, of course, could hear me lose control of my emotions out in the hall and that alone hurt him immeasurably, but he was also devastated because he loved my Holly too.

I told him that I was grateful beyond words for what he did for her as well as me, even though it cost him dearly.

We talked a bit longer, and then he excused himself and went into the house.

He came out with a card that he said he had been holding onto for a while but this seemed to be the appropriate time to give to me.

It wasn't in an envelope or even signed, but it said, "No matter how crazy my life gets, I know you'll be there, and when it's your turn to lose it… you can count on me." On the inside: "We're so screwed if it happens at the same time."

We talked for another hour or so, and then I excused myself and went into the house.

When I came back out, I turned my chair to face him, sat back down and something profound like, "I have always loved you, and I love you now, even though you are going through these difficult times and are feeling so upset and depressed about so many devastating events going on in your life and you feel unlovable, and not worthy of anything."

I slipped something into his hand and asked, "Will you marry me?"

We talked for a minute more then I asked him again, "Will you marry me? If you will, then put the ring on my finger," I held out my left hand, palm side down.

"But, if you're not ready yet, then put the ring in this hand," I held out my right hand, palm side up. "Either is perfectly ok to me."

He slipped the ring on my finger. It was the same three-emerald ring I got for myself to celebrate the three-year anniversary in our first marriage that never was to be.

It was an amazing night.

"Caveman No Like Dentist"

I finally made Paulie a dentist appointment because he wasn't doing it and I was tired of asking.

Wednesday night there was a message on the machine at home, "Your wife made you an appointment for the 19th, but we have a cancellation. Would you like to come in Friday at 2PM?"

I heard him shout at the machine, "I am not superstitious, but there is no way I'm sitting in a dentist's chair on Friday the 13th!"

He was actually yelling at the machine, as if the woman who left the message could hear him.

Big, tough Caveman also spook at full moon.

"Dream Come True"

Paulie had been seriously laid up with severe back pain since Saturday, getting worse every day.

Finally, I took him to the doctor who realized that Paulie had really strained his lumbar muscles badly, but fortunately, not hurt ligaments or nerves. None the less, he was waylaid with heavy medications and stayed home for the rest of the week staring at the ceiling on bed rest.

That whole day went something like this: "Let me help you with that." "No, I'm fine; I can do it myself... ouch..."

That degraded to this the next day: "Let me help you with that." "No, I'm fine; I can do it myself... ouch ouch ouch..."

Predictably it became this: "Let me help you with that." "No, I'm fine; I can do it myself... Oh holy crap!!! Help me! Hurry, hurry, hurry!"

His pain was so bad this morning that I had to help him out of the shower, dry him off and dress him.

He said he never really understood how hard or how often we laughed together until this happened and quickly discovered that even laughter brought sharp flashes of pain.

But, there's still no reason not to make him laugh, you know, even though it causes him extreme agony. I'm fine with that.

Just for, well, giggles actually, I said, "Laughter is the best medicine." That started an avalanche of laughter and he had to brace himself for the pain by digging his fingers into the couch.

Late last night, or early this morning (it's a blur), he turned to me in bed after suddenly waking up and he panted, "I just had a horrible dream."

"What was it about?"

He gritted his teeth in pain, "You."

I'm thinking, "Why is that a bad thing?" but yawned and asked him to tell me about it anyway.

"I dreamed you were running to me and jumped into my arms!"

I started laughing, which made him laugh, but then he saw the glint in my eye and all of the blood drained from his face.

"Oh, no. *WHAT?*"

"Oh, honey, it was only a dream, but it could still happen."

His body actually convulsed as he tried not to laugh, but I wasn't finished.

"Paulie, I love you so much, that I will try my hardest to make sure that *all* of your dreams come true."

Today, he's not skipping his pain meds.

"The Future Becomes Now"

While getting ready for our trip to Texas last month, I spotted Paulie's carry-on bag.

Right on top of it was my old CD player and earphones (remember he's a caveman, so no iPod, right?).

I picked it up, went into the living room where he was, waved it in the air and said, "You aren't planning on tuning me out, are you?"

Honest to God, people, he looked up at me and said, "What?"

"$3.02"

Paulie and I are living pretty close to the bone.

He's got two jobs and my hours at work were cut to thirty-five per week. If the economy doesn't improve in a month or two, they will return our hours to forty per week and lay people off.

We are fine, though. We see this as something to use laughter to get us through. Don't misunderstand me, there have been tears, and sleepless nights, but together, we laugh.

We have always alternated weeks on shopping, cooking, and cleanup in the kitchen, but for my weeks I no longer have money to buy food for us.

Last week, after my bills were paid, I had $3.02 with nothing left over for food. I was happy to be in the black rather than in the dreaded red, but this was tough.

He's been eating ingredients from the back of our pantry like olives, Jell-O, tuna, some horrid cheap chili and the dreaded Spam (his favorite).

I wanted to buy some jam so I could have PB & Js for breakfast and lunch (cereal for dinner), but I couldn't afford a jar, so I started eating peanut butter sandwiches.

Motoring along on that for a few days, and I started to run out of bread.

Yesterday morning, I was looking forward to peanut butter on the one remaining hot dog bun in the bread basket, when Paulie called me into the kitchen and said, "Look!" I looked. Strawberry preserves. And Bread. And milk. Ohhh.

Paulie and I definitely look out for each other. When one of us is sick, the other takes over. He's working two jobs, so I finished his week of chores (we switch weeks for laundry and vacuuming too). When one of us is short on money, the other provides.

I'm not trying to worry people. I'm just trying to say that things are rough, but we are still laughing.

It doesn't fix a damn thing, but it brings us closer together in the struggle.

It's how we roll.

Days later…

If you're having a gray day, like we are here in Washington, then this will cheer you up, at least for the length of a chuckle.

I got a piece of PB & J stuck in my throat and yarked up about a half cup of water that had a flavored mix in it. It was still chilled and most of it exited pretty violently through my nose.

First time for *that* and I don't care to ever repeat it. Also, no sign of the P, B, and/or J, but all is well…

Too much information? Ok, well here's a nice thought to leave you with…

Yesterday on my way to work, I had a bald eagle fly parallel to my car for about a mile, and a few miles after that there was a full grown buck just outside the tree line.

I love this place.

"Cookie-Of-The-Month"

For this month's Cookie-of-the-Month (I'm baking a different cookie every month for fun at home), I chose thumbprint cookies. These are tiny teacake balls rolled in crushed pecans, then, after you push your thumb through the middle, you fill up the dent you just made with a dollop of your favorite jam or preserves. Paulie's a fruitoholic, so I used blackberry preserves for the first batch.

They are in and out of the oven in no time. I pushed a dozen onto a little plate and handed them off to him in the living room to taste-test.

He was instantly disappointed that they weren't gigantic gooey chocolate cookies that would take a whole gallon of ice-cold milk to get down.

I growled, "Try one."

We both had one at the same time, and I really liked mine.

I left the plate with him and went to retrieve another batch from the oven.

After my second cookie, I said from the kitchen, "They are surprisingly filling and quite yummy, actually."

He brought the (almost) empty plate back and said, "Yeah, I know. Leave these in here because I still need room for lunch."

I had to break the news to Paulie that next year I am going to do a Cake-of-the-Month, and then the year after that, a Pie-of-the-Month.

I didn't hear any dissent (like that matters), so it's a go.

Woo hoo!

Years later…

A few years ago, I did a Cookie-of-the-Month. I baked twelve different kinds of cookies that year, and for the next year I was going to the same thing, but with cakes.

When it got towards the end of the year of cookies, I reminded Paulie of my plan. He vehemently declined my offer, "Oh, please for the love of God, no!" When I asked him why not, he said it was because *he would eat them*.

Months later I made a cake for a United Way auction. It was made with a pint of rocky road (ice cream of my choice) in the batter. I made it as a Bundt cake, with homemade chocolate sauce poured all over it, and full-sized marshmallows floating high on the pooling chocolate sauce in hole the middle of the cake ring.

When it was finished, I stood back and beamed at its beauty.

I received lots of ohhhs and ahhhs from work and a thumbs-up from the auction winner.

When I got home I renewed my bid to make a cake a month for us, but Paulie, who was staring wide-eyed at a picture of the United Way cake, groaned and once again said, "Oh please, no. For the love of God, no!"

"Caveman No Like 21st Century"

Paulie has been ever the faithful caveman with new-fangled things like cell phones (we don't have any), iPods (we don't have any, he uses my old CD player because his tape player broke), hot new options in cars like cruise control, and now voice mail (we had to give up our answering machine).

He's pitching a fit because he has to pick up the phone and punch in *99 to check voicemail. "I hope this is worth it to you," he growled.

"Well, considering it took me three days and a few over-seas phone calls to set up the phone /internet/ wireless/ splitter/ router/ modem/ new laptop/ Windows 7 connections, I hope so too."

To make him completely boil over, I told him he could also check voicemail online.

Wow, that tantrum was awesome to witness.

It still makes me giggle.

"In Sickness"

Paulie and I are near the end of our Anniversary Week for celebrating our 10th wedding anniversary. This little vacation was on me because he paid to get my car fixed when mouse poop was discovered on my engine block (it was a cold winter and the little critter climbed in there to stay warm and, for entertainment, it chewed on some wires).

We were going to do a day trip east, another south, and a day trip out west to the San Juan Islands (Wednesday, Thursday, Friday). Paulie loves to drive and we love to get out and just go, even if our plans change. Changed plans are usually a good thing on our road trips.

For Day One, I got us a room at Tulalip Casino and Resort.

That's as far as we went.

The hotel and our room were beautiful, but as we walked through the casino after check-in we discovered that neither one of us gamble. I put a fiver in and a few minutes later got $7.50 out, but have no idea why. The slot machines are more like computer games, these days, than old-time Vegas one-arm-bandits. No romance, just a hungry mouth to feed.

We moved on, and by the time we left the casino for the dining rooms we were hacking from the smoke inhalation. Ok, so casinos are out. Good to know. But, there's still the resort!

We ate at a wonderful buffet, then, being sailors, we bellied up to the bar and ordered drinks like Sammy Hagar's Cabo Wabo tequila, Long Island Iced Tea, Alien Secretions, Rusty Nail, Johnny Walker Blue, Otter Pop, Quaalude, and (quite) a few others, plus lots and lots of water.

Because it was mid-week and fairly early in the day, we were very nearly the only ones there in the bar. Stephanie, our bartender, served us well, so we left happy.

We then went upstairs to cap off the evening with some, uh, *marital relations.*

The next day, we were not hung-over. At all.

But, at about 5:30 in the morning, Paulie decided that the trip was over.

He had become violently ill with the latest and greatest influenza (yes, he had the flu shot).

He had chills, nausea, his sinuses were flooded, he had gastrointestinal distress, body weakness - the whole nine yards.

We checked out very early and I drove us home. As soon as I got him to bed, I unpacked, started laundry and checked in on him.

Not that there was any doubt in my mind that he was sick, but seeing him in bed fully clothed in sweats and socks with the room heat on high was rather shocking. This man walks in snow barefoot and wears shorts in nineteen degree weather.

He stayed cocooned for days. This was bad.

Yesterday, I got a fresh set of clothes laid out for him, and told him to get out of bed and take a shower.

"You are so mean."

"No, my love, I'm going to wash the bedclothes. When it's done, you'll be de-scummed, wearing clean clothes and have a fresh place to lay your head. I'm taking care of you."

Nurses. Sheesh.

Although our fabulous little vacation was blown to bits, I told him that all was well and that this is the "in sickness and in health" part of the marriage. And I told him I loved him very much.

Fortunately, I had already given him his anniversary gift. He opened it as soon as we got to our room at the resort. I started the video camera because I knew that his reaction was going to be pure gold.

The envelope said, "I know that this isn't an anniversary card, but it's what's inside that counts, right?" He ripped into it and out popped a $25 Red Lobster gift card.

He sees the commercials all the time and just drools because, and here's the kicker folks, there's not a Red Lobster within four hundred miles of our house.

Happy anniversary!

"Laughter is the Best Medicine"

A few weeks ago, Paulie was stomping around the house, grumbling at everything, and then he went to bed.

The next morning when he came downstairs, I said to him, "You lied to me."

Well, if he wasn't *grrr* before, then he was most definitely *grrr* now because we just don't lie to each other, so therefore he was being falsely accused.

Ready for a fight, in his bad mood, he shot back, "Really? How's that?"

"You said that your back was feeling much better, but when you are in pain you are quite a *prick*, ergo, you are not feeling better. You lied."

My blatant name-calling (something else we don't do) cracked a smile and from there, no matter how hard he tried, he couldn't stop a belly laugh.

He behaved the rest of the day.

Sometimes, laughter *is* the best medicine.

For my part, not everything is worth fighting for or about. If I hadn't been paying attention and just got pissed, then we'd both be fighting for no reason. I was just going to hold my tongue until he felt better, but I don't like him saying that he feels fine when actually he's in a lot of pain.

He doesn't have to hide it from me.

That doesn't mean I won't go airborne and land on him when he's stretched out on the couch, but the chances of this happening decrease if I know he's already in pain. But not by much.

"Story Telling"

We celebrated Paulie's birthday over at the Burton Clanhouse with lots of food and lots (four generations) of family.

The subject of movies came up and a cousin asked me why I have so many (over 1,500).

My usual answer is that I love story-telling which is why I also have so many books.

Instead of saying that, though, I said, "I have a theory about that. I think that if I didn't have so many movies, I'd be spending a lot more time with Paulie sharing, uh, *marital relations*. But whenever there's a break in our schedules and I'm thinking of this subject, a new movie magically appears and Paulie's saying to me, 'Look! Look! I just put in a new movie for you!' and to me, that's like a shiny object I've just got to stare at, so I forget the whole reason I hunted him down in the first place."

To my right, I saw Paulie looking very uncomfortable for bringing up this subject matter at the dinner table (but nodding his head none-the-less), then I heard, on my left, his octogenarian grandmother choke on her drink.

When she could breathe again, she was laughing.

God, I love this family!

"Cars Are Not Submarines"

Paulie, who rarely does anything bone-headed, drove his Subaru past two "Street Flooded" signs and into a stream that was crossing over the roadway.

It was at the very end of his paper route (his second job) one day years ago at about 6AM.

He called me at home and said that I needed to come pick him up because his "engine flooded" and his car stalled. I told him I'd be ready for work soon, and just come get him and he could take my car for the rest of the day.

When I get there I see the road signs, and then I see his car dead on the road, and then I see him and notice that his pants are wet way up passed his knees.

I ask, "How exactly did your car's engine flood?"

He said, "When the water came up over the hood."

This actually made me speechless.

I finally asked, "Were you tired or was this testosterone?"

He chose "tired" and I believe him because he just doesn't do this kind of thing.

I said, "You are now aware that your car is not amphibious?"

Long story short, we are now calling her Ariel after the Disney mermaid who gave up her fins for feet, "Water's bad for Ariel, Paulie. Okay?"

He later called me at work sounding really down. He's going to have to start a claim with his insurance and they are going to send a guy out to check the damages for an estimate, but Paulie got really disturbed when they said it might be a total loss.

I replied, "Calm down, that's actually what we should be hoping for." He was utterly perplexed.

I told him that it's already and eleven-year-old car. He doesn't really want to sink (no pun intended) a few thousand dollars to get an eleven-year-old car back on its feet (pun intended). If it's a total loss then the insurance company will cut him a check and he can go buy himself a brand new used car.

He groaned.

"That's one of the reasons for car insurance. Understand?"

"No, but I believe you. I'm going to go lie down now..."

As it turned out, the car was a total loss and insurance did not pay.

Months later, after Paulie got a new used car, things didn't get much better.

He did all of the research for it on line and then went down to Seattle with his uncle to do the test drives and chose which car to get.

When he got home I said, "Don't tell me what color it is yet, but I hope it's gray because I'm going to call it "The Rock". You need to remember that cars don't usually swim, they sink."

He grumbled or mumbled something.

"Ok," I said, "What color is it?"

He said, "It's gray".

The Rock turned out to be a dud and permanently broke down just days after he brought it home. It's going to take him years to pay it off.

"The Fire Department & Root Beer"

I had a "suspicious" mole scare during my annual physical. It was punch-biopsied and later determined to be harmless. I got the good news by phone yesterday.

More good news: because of my medical training, when the time comes, I can professionally remove my own stitches.

Anyway, after the mild freak-out, and the relief of the "all clear," I shook off the heebie-jeebies and moved on.

Part of the monotony of life includes laundry. I did a load, then for some reason, wanted to run a rinse cycle on it again. That's something I never do. There was smoke, and a burning wire smell.

Fearing fire with all of the lint on the floor under the unit, I called the fire department. Two very cute Bellingham firefighters came and pulled the stacked washer/dryer out of the hall closet.

The water hose became disconnected and started draining the washer tub full of water all over my entry way.

Three of us did a chain-gang of pitchers and my chili pot to dump the rest of the water that was ready to spill.

By the way, there was still a pretty red fire truck parked outside of my apartment building that still contained firefighters waiting for these two to finish up with this huge emergency.

Soon, a third firefighter popped in with a hose to syphon water directly from the washer tub. He sucked on the hose and choked on my Downey-flavored-hopefully-clean water that had been soaking my hopefully clean clothes. Yikes.

I had locked the cats in my bedroom. All of my windows and doors were open to get rid of the smoke and horrid smell. There were firefighter helmets and meters and tools all over the place. Soaked towels; pots and pans; puddles of water. It was fun.

I thanked them repeatedly and told them not to worry about the still wet floor. One of them kept trying to dry everything and was worried about the water under the washer.

"Thank you, I feel better now that the apartment won't burn down in the middle of the night." I shook their hands, thanked them again and they left.

So, I couldn't do laundry this weekend, and now had soaked towels and a whole load of soaked clothes to fret over, but now it was time to eat.

All I had was yogurt, so I ordered a pizza and a two-liter bottle of root beer. The pizza arrived cold and the root beer was warm, but I was bound and determined to eat, drink, and be merry.

I settled into my chair, grabbed the root beer and twisted the top clean off.

It exploded all over me, the chair, the pizza, the remote controls, the table, the phone, the lamp, the blanket, my glasses…

Weeks later (well, not really *weeks*)…

Yeah, I pulled the stitches out too early. The next day at work, I knelt down and felt something pop open. Bleeding occurred, soaking my pant leg.

On my way out the door to go home and change, a friend stopped me, "Jeez Julie, what happened?"

I looked down at my leg, with the blood still flowing freely, and said, "I pulled the stitches out too early."

"Why'd you take your stitches out?"

"Because it was fun."

No response. I looked up from the gore and saw her staring at me. I said, "I guess I misunderstood the question."

She pointed, "You're bleeding all down your leg!"

"Yeah, I think these pants are ruined."

She looked at me as if I had lost my mind. "Are you going to get the stitches put back in?"

"No, just going home to change clothes and do a patch job."

She walked away shaking her head.

So, I went home and soaked what are probably going to become my summer shorts, which is unfortunate, because they were my favorite pair of pants. Then I found a wad of cotton balls, clear packaging tape and alcohol swabs, performed a brilliant "field dressing," jumped into my least favorite pair of pants in case the bandage leaked, and went back to work.

The same coworker came up to ask me how I bandaged myself up.

"Household products… various household products." Beaming, I proudly showed her my excellent dressing - no leaks. Woo hoo!

Again, she was shocked.

"Hey, it's not like I used my hot glue gun or my staple gun."

She said, "Julie, you are *without a doubt*, the strangest woman I have *ever* known." I naturally had to say "thank you" to that.

Scare is over…

Washer's fixed…

Stitches are pulled…

Pants are not stained…

Still finding spots of root beer…

"Guest Speaker"

I'm still meeting people at my new job as the assistant to the assistant to the Chair of Pathology.

The other day the entire campus got e-mail about an unfortunate mishap of an instructor who spilled soda on the podium thereby ruining the electrical circuits and microphone creating about four thousand dollars' worth of damage. No name was given, but everyone was officially warned to never bring food or drink to the podium again.

Yesterday the big boss came around to introduce me to a very important guest. I stood up and shook his hand when they came to my desk.

My boss was being very serious, telling me that this gentleman was the head medical examiner for five counties and that the United Nations, US Government, and foreign governments all called on him regularly for his extensive expertise at crash sites and natural disasters.

Without interrupting my boss, who was going on and on about this guy's credentials, his guest leaned over my desk and whispered to me, "I'm the one who spilled the soda on the podium."

I burst out laughing and kept giggling with him as my boss continued on with my new friend's apparent high intelligence and monumental importance to mere mortals...

"Saturday, September 2, 1989"

JULIE ANN MCCULLOCH WEDS TERRY LEE ALDRIDGE.

Twenty-one years ago today, Terry Lee Aldridge and I married. I was 20, and he was ten years my senior.

The marriage lasted less than a year, although we never divorced. I was incredibly immature and terribly naive about important things like relationships and money. I was very mature in other ways, but these two particular lessons do come about at a rather heavy price, don't they?

We met when I was 18. He had come in to rescue the restaurant I was working at from going under. I was dating someone else, but

Terry and I were both interested in photography, so things progressed from there.

After we moved in together he was diagnosed with a previously misdiagnosed testicular cancer.

He had surgery and radiation and was given a clean bill of health, but he never made it out of the five-year cancer-free window. After we married, it came back and killed him. He was just 33 years old.

As I said, though, soon after we married, the marriage was over. I joined the Navy and kept in touch. We were still very, very good friends with no desire to divorce and wished nothing but the best for each other. His live-in girlfriend, in fact, got really freaked out because I was nice to her when she answered his phone. Funny as hell though. When she handed the phone off to him, we laughed about it.

I remember getting the call that the cancer was back. I was stationed in San Diego. I was devastated.

By the time I got to Hawaii we knew that the end was near. I begged him to come live with me there so I could take care of him, but he said he wanted to stay with his doctors in North Carolina. I spoke with him two days before he died. I called him husband, he called me wife. Then he was gone.

That same year, I met Paulie.

" First Date "

OUR FIRST DATE WAS A PEARL JAM CONCERT ON SEPTEMBER
25, 1992, AT THE UNIVERSITY OF HAWAII'S AMPHITHEATER,
THEN DRINKS AT HONOLULU'S CLUB C-5.

Paulie and I met in the Navy in Hawaii.

I've got a picture that was taken on our first date, and I can see it in my eyes that I knew then that he was the love of my life. It took him *seventeen years* and two painful divorces to figure out that I was, and always had been, the love of his. I was the safe, warm, loving home he'd been searching for, and had offered him all along.

About a decade after that first date, we were both out of the Navy, and he brought me to his home-town of Bellingham, Washington to marry him.

He introduced me to his beloved grandmother who loved me immediately because I was wearing purple shoes.

We were sitting on the couch in her purple house, with Paulie between us, when I told her (jokingly) that I was only marrying him for his money.

She sucked in her breath, leaned over his lap and whispered to me (seriously), "He doesn't have any."

"Oh, damn," I kept going with the joke, "I guess I'll have to marry him for love, then."

With that, she got a glint in her eye and giggled.

Within a year, we were married, and two years after that, he divorced me.

But, he came back.

And after seventeen years of fearing the power of love, he came back to me, for the last time, to stay.

"Chocolate Mocha Cheesecake for United Way"

To raise money for the United Way, my office held a bake sale.

I auctioned off three cakes to be baked within the next twelve months, whenever the winner requested one. The winning bid was $44. Whew, pressure!

For a potluck for her department, she chose the Chocolate Mocha Cheesecake. I'm baking it now. Ah, this had better be good!

Actually, the winner is extremely nice, but I really want to do well. That's hard to do with a cake I've never done before (it's my first cheesecake too), and on a limited budget (no do-overs), for a bunch of people who actually love food (it's for the FDA department, in fact).

The good news is, Paulie's working tonight so there won't be any track marks from him running his fingers through the soft chocolate creamcheese cake before I hand it off to the winner tomorrow morning.

On top of the cake in chocolate chips, I put "MMM..." as in "good". I hope I spelled it correctly.

I made a little sign to go with it, "Chocolate Mocha Cheesecake ingredient list (check your diet at the door): Devil's food cake (for the crust), butter, eggs, creamcheese, sweetened condensed milk, sour cream, vanilla, coffee, semi-sweet chocolate... and the pan was greased wall-to-wall with Crisco"

Wish me luck!

Later that day...

The CHOCOLATE MOCHA CHEESECAKE was an incredible SUCCESS!!! I now like it BETTER than TIRAMISU. I'm not a mocha LOVER because I dislike COFFEE, but I'VE ALWAYS LOVED

TIRAMISU. But now I love this CHEESECAKE better. It got RAVE reviews from the FDA department AT WORK, so I tried it myself in case they were just trying to MAKE ME FEEL GOOD. I thought it was INCREDIBLE. I NOW like it BETTER THAN TIRAMISU. This is me on CAFFEINE!!!!! I now like MOCHA. My favorite mocha dish is chocolate mocha cheesecake. I LIKE IT BETTER THAN TIRAMISU.

I'll stop now. Mostly because I think I'm now hooked on CAFFEINE and NEED TO FIND SOME MORE. Maybe I should make up some MOCHA! You know. Like in a cheesecake. MMM…

And later that year…

I made brownies for last United Way fundraiser this year.

I thought of using a muffin tin rather than a big 9x11 pan. No cupcake papers, so I just spooned the batter into the greased muffin holders. I've never done it like that before.

Then I thought of what would taste good jammed in the middle of each, so I cut up little squares of creamcheese and unwrapped some caramels. I had one of each flavor a few nights ago for the trial run before I made them last night for the fundraiser.

The little brownies barely rose above the pan, so there was no muffin-type top to them and when I bit into each they were solid (heavy) and chewy rather than cake like. Oh man, were they good.

The judging was People's Choice this time (usually, it's the supervisors). So fellow UPSers bought which ever brownies they wanted (there were more than fifteen entries so multiply that out by at least five servings each) for one dollar each, and for every one you bought, you got one vote. I bought five, so I got five votes and I voted all on one coworker.

I emailed her to tell her that her presentation was fantastic and that the flavor was completely outstanding and that I hoped she'd win.

She, in turn, told me that she really tried hard to find the perfect recipe because she was so inspired by my chocolate mocha cheesecake. I got all misty-eyed on that note of praise, let me tell you

I'm not sure how much was raised for United Way, but I will tell you this: she won!

"Still No Slam"

Paulie told me the other day that he was interested in getting his RN. He's always shrugged off the idea, so it was nice to hear him say it.

I replied, "Aw, sweetie, I'm already so very proud of you as an LPN, I can't imagine what'd happen if you became a registered nurse."

As it is now, I introduce him like, "This is my husband Paulie, he's a nurse." Later he would say, "That waitress really didn't need to know I'm a nurse."

If he became a registered nurse, I'd probably start saying, "Hi I'm Julie, and this is my husband. He's an RN." He'd have to say, "Hi, I'm Paul." "Oh yeah, sorry honey. And his name is Paul."

It's damn convenient to have him around. Every once in a while I'll ask him things like, "What's the maximum amount of acetaminophen I can take in a day?" He'll immediately have an answer.

Days ago I asked him which vitamin I needed to take to help me with leg cramps I sometimes get in the middle of the night. I'm drinking plenty of water, so anything after that stumps me.

I started my query by saying, "Nurse Betty...?"

He interrupted, "It's Nurse Ratchet to you." This turned out to be our play on Louise Fletcher's character.

"Hey, I'm not cuckoo."

He looked at me.

I looked at him.

He continued to look at me.

I caved, "Oh, all right, you got me there. Now just answer the question."

He did, but honestly I didn't hear him or even remember a thing he said because I was focused on trying to come up with a slam to his *One Flew Over the Cuckoo's Nest* reference.

I never got one because I was sidetracked by a shiny object.

Then a swarm of butterflies came by and I had to go find my net and chase them around the yard.

In my jammies

Most of that is a true story. Actually, it's all true except for the last half-dozen lines or so. I think he said to take potassium for leg cramps and I wasn't distracted by a shiny object (that time, anyway).

I do think I was wearing jammies though.

Still no slam, but I'll get him.

Thank you for spending these days with me.

Nothing is every boring in *A Day in the Life if Julie.*

And now, if you dare, read on.

And now a few stories from

"The Book of Dammit"

"Famous Last Words"

For four months late last year, I worked my tail off moving from a couch-potato to a competent exerciser.

I walked over forty miles on the treadmill given to us by Uncle Jim and Aunt Marge, and counted over a thousand sit-ups.

Paulie was completely quiet about my whole trek until my Christmas card went out to them where I repeated, yet again, thanks for the machine. "I am so grateful! I use it all the time!" Before the envelope was sealed, he wrote on the card, "Yeah, but she still weighs the same!"

Dammit.

I have been stuck at this weight ever since I lost the 22 pounds after the Lap-Band surgery three years ago. I could seriously pig out (as much as the band allows, of course) for a week as I did on our anniversary last year, and step on the scale with trepidation, only to realize I am exactly the same weight. Or, I could be a couch-potato. Or, as in this case, I could work out for months. Always the same weight. Really, really weird.

Yes, the scale works because it shows Paulie's weight is going up. Hilarious.

To bite back, I tried to embarrass him when his uncle and brother came over for a visit.

Paulie is actually quite shameless, so trying to embarrass him, and in front of family no less, is an up-hill battle but I'm convinced that one day this dream of mine will come true. You need stealth to get something past him because he has a sharp mind. Not always a good thing!

Anyway, the four of us were talking about my lack of weight loss after so much effort to be non-couch-potatoed when I tried to get the last word in and I said to Paulie, "Well, at least I can see my own pubic hair!"

I should have forewarned you that things are never mature when it's boy's night at the Burton house, and I always fit in well on boy's night.

Paulie immediately fired back, "Hey, I can see your pubic hair, too."

Dammit!

"90s Woman"

AFTER PASS-IN-REVIEW, WITH MY MOM, FEBRUARY, 1990.

The Navy was very good for me. I felt very empowered from boot camp until my very last day in the service nearly five years later.

Although the Armed Services had come a long way, I still served with a few men who felt that "*girls*" didn't belong in the Navy, so I worked even harder to prove to them that I deserved to be there, that it was my right, and that I could pull my own weight and take care of not only myself but others as well. I found this easy to do because I believe what a woman may do and will do is not directly related to what she can do; it is directly related to what she *allowed* to do.

After my discharge in the mid-1990s, I settled in New England. I was a proud American, I was a proud veteran and I was a proud woman. I was strong and confident and was sure I could do anything for and by myself. I called myself a "90s Woman".

My first year in Massachusetts, there was a blizzard, and I drove the car I bought on a tropical island through it with new-found skill.

One day, mid-winter, I was out running errands and figuring I could "up my game," I stopped to get my nails done before I went to visit family friends. When I came out of the salon, it was snowing. Hard. Sideways.

Taking a deep, calming breath, I got behind the wheel and decided this little storm was not going to stop me. I got out of the shopping center all right, traffic was fine, and I was taking it slow and easy, just like a smart 90s Woman should.

While slowing down on rural route in Wrentham to pull into a driveway, I undershot the turn on the slick road and ditched myself.

"Ok, ok, this is ok. It's a shallow ditch, just see if you can back out or rock it back and forth to get out. Stay calm. You know you can do this." I couldn't. I was stuck. I already had my flashers on and was about to abandon the car and call for a tow.

All of a sudden, emerging from the white-out, a pickup truck pulls into the driveway I was aiming for and stops. Three gorgeous men pop out, drop sand behind my tires, and tell me to pull out slowly, and after I did they all jumped back into their truck and vanished back into the storm.

The whole time, I'm yelling out my driver's side window, *over and over again*, "I'd come out and help, but my nails are wet!"

I successfully pulled into my friend's driveway, parked my car, and before I burst out laughing, I screamed, "I'd come out and help, but my nails are wet???"

Dammit!

"Mammoth Ivory"

Ok, I have another one for you but this time, it wasn't me.

Soon after I started at UPS, a smart, kind and gentle coworker said that she liked my earrings.

I replied, "Thank you. These are probably my favorite pair because they were made with the ivory from the tusk of a mammoth."

She wondered out loud, "Oh, I hope they didn't hurt the poor thing."

I briefly pondered my choices of how to break the news to my friend when I settled with this: I cupped my hands around my mouth and spoke as if into a bullhorn, *Mammoths are extinct animals!*

She sucked in a deep breath, turned a brand-new shade of red, and I didn't hear it, but I saw her thinking...

Dammit.

"Defensive Driving"

To move my life from Texas to Washington State after I accepted the proposal from the man I'd known and loved for years, we had to rent a huge moving van which, in turn was hauling a trailer behind it that held my car.

Paulie did most of the driving, but I said I wanted a turn at it but didn't want to do it on the highway because it was my first time with something this big on the road.

On the side roads, behind the wheel, I checked the mirrors, the steering and the brake situation.

Once I was fairly comfortable, he started pointing to stuff on the dashboard and making comments about my driving.

Getting instantly defensive, I growled, "Hey, mister, back off! I'm doing fine. Just because I'm a *girl*, it doesn't mean I need advice from you about driving a truck!"

He started to respond when I stopped him cold, "What makes you so damn sure of yourself anyway? What's the biggest thing you've ever driven?"

"A submarine."

A nuclear. US Navy. Fast attack. Submarine.

Dammit.

"Creamcheesed"

Paulie's perfecting his cream cheese frosting recipe.

I said, "For the love of all things holy, please bake a cake to put under it this time," otherwise, he'll just eat the freshly whipped frosting right out of the bowl. With a spoon. As if it was oatmeal. *Yelch!*

And now there's a cake with home-made cream cheese frosting in the fridge. Instead of keeping the sweets in a form that only he would eat, there's now a cake that I would eat.

I just got finished losing six more pounds.

Dammit.

"Caveman No Wear Glasses"

Paulie went to the eye doctor last weekend.

Aside from the Navy, it was the first time in his adult life he'd ever had his eyes checked.

I was hoping for glasses.

In the chair, the doc asked him, "Well, what brings you here today?"

My caveman replied, "My wife made me."

The doctor seemed nonplused, so Paulie inquired.

The ophthalmologist simply said, "Yeah, we get that a lot. Now cover your right eye…"

Well, Caveman no wear glasses. He *barely* needs reading glasses.

He smirked, so I said, "Yeah, good for you. And now back to the dentist…"

Dammit!

"A Dammit Story From Grandma"

Paulie's grandma is a fantastic lady. The matriarch of the Burton clan married once to the love of her life, and has been widowed for a quarter of a century.

The woman loves all things purple, and still drives herself to church in a purple Grand Am.

She lives with her son and daughter-in-law in what I've affectionately titled the "Clanhouse" and still cooks up a storm on holidays (so does Uncle Jim, by the way, so even though you firmly believe you will never eat again, you never, ever, *ever* leave empty handed).

At the dinner table Grandma's a lively talker and can contribute a lot more now that she has her new and improved hearing aid.

One time she was telling us all about a man from her church who apparently wanted to court her. She said, "Ewww," to us.

Everyone at the table nodded their heads.

Another time she talked a bit about a woman from her church. She said, "The woman is just so old! I think she must be eighty!"

Everyone at the table looked at each other.

"Uh, Mom?"

"Hmmm?"

"You're eighty-two."

Although life is full of *Dammit* stories, I only have one more for you.

Enjoy.

"Colored Socks"

When Paulie and I first married ten years ago, we had an informal wedding. Casual, because Caveman no wear ties.

And we had it outside, because neither one of us is affiliated with any church, temple, synagogue or mosque.

It was a relaxed event. Well, that day was, anyway.

A few weeks before The Day, I brought home a set of three pairs of men's colored sox: one pair was tan, another dark khaki and the last pair was chocolate brown.

I invited him to pick what color he was going to wear, and I'd choose from the other two.

It was as if I was telling him some unbelievably horrific news that he just couldn't bear to hear. "Colored socks? *Colored socks?* I'm not wearing any colored socks!"

I said, "Now you listen here mister! We are getting married in jeans and flannel shirts out on a dock on a lake! If you don't want to wear the colored socks, you can go rent a tuxedo and I'll start looking into which church can marry us the soonest! You didn't have to wear them before but after that outburst, *you damn well better wear them now!*"

The silence was deafening as he tried to figure a way out of the muck he had just stepped in.

I could see him thinking… He then picked the lightest pair, and after our wedding I never saw them again.

On the way out of the room with his hated cargo I heard the magic word.

Dammit!

PS – He hates this story.

And now from the book

"MS'd Up: Adventures

in Multiple Sclerosis"

"Honor. And No Shame."

I have MS: Relapsing/Remitting multiple sclerosis, to be exact.

As I understand it, this is a *progressive* (the damage adds up as the years go by), *auto-immune disease* (my body's defense system is attacking its own healthy tissue), *of the central nervous system* (brain and spinal cord), *with an unknown etiology* (no known cause), *and no known cure.*

Specifically, during a relapse, my immune system attacks the myelin sheath (fatty, protective layer around the tails of certain neurons – it's the "white matter" that surrounds the "gray matter" in the brain), stripping it, causing the signal to misfire. Think of a lamp with a wire that has had some of the insulation cut away. With this damage, the lamp might still work well, or it might blink on and off, or even turn off and stay off forever.

At the onset of the relapse, I go to the emergency room at the Seattle VA hospital. There I'm given three days of steroids (to decrease the inflammation at the affected site) in the form of solumedrol intervenes infusion. Then I go home for a few more weeks of high dosages of a steroid called prednisone. With all of my relapses over the last seven years, by the time I am weaned of the medicine, my symptoms have all gone into remission.

With this damage to the lamp cord, as with the damage to the myelin sheath, it can be repaired. Perhaps the lamp needs some electrical tape. Perhaps my body can heal its assaulted wound. Maybe the tape didn't fix the lamp, and it's permanently damaged. Maybe my body couldn't fix it either, and the damaged wire is scared over. This scaring is called sclerosis. Maybe this isn't the first scar. Maybe there are multiple.

This scaring can be seen on a MRI. With this magnetic resonance imaging the doctor can see old scaring as well as newer damage. I've seen the images, and can see the white spots and streaks of the scars (called plaques), but that's the most I understand about it.

I am thankful that I get an annual MRI at the VA, free of charge. They take very good care of me there. My emergency room visits, lodging during the procedures and the steroids are free. The daily subcutaneous injections I give myself to lessen both the severity and frequency of the relapses are very, very inexpensive because I get them at the VA. I am very lucky, and I don't ever forget that. I am very grateful, and I have never, ever felt anything other than grateful, since my diagnosis on Thanksgiving Day, 2002.

For my first known lapse, so to speak, the front part of my right thigh started to go numb as if shot with Novocain. Then, within an hour, the numbness spread around my thigh, and within days it started spidering up and down my leg, torso and arm. The sensation loss intensified and filled in until it went from my toes up to my arm pit.

Because there is no test to diagnose MS, they run tests to rule-out other diseases. MS was suspected, but until another relapse happened, it couldn't be proclaimed, and because of the behavior of my symptoms and that they were all only one side, the differential diagnosis was transverse myelitis. I was treated, the symptoms went away, and I went on with my life.

Within the year, I had another relapse. This, along with the plaques showing up on my MRI, proved MS. I remember I was in my hospital bed, lunch had just been served, and my doctor came in and told me. After he left, I stared at the Thanksgiving pumpkin pie on the food tray and thought about my future.

I was given a choice of medications. One is called Copaxone, and is a daily subcutaneous injection that leaves bee-sting welts at the injection site (my tummy). The other was a class of interferons which had side-effects I didn't like, so I chose the first option.

Years and relapses and remissions go by, and then...

This latest episode with multiple sclerosis presented itself a couple of weeks ago when I felt my lips and gums go numb in a series of waves over a day or two, but it never stayed "solid", I chose to ignore it and then it all went away. This was all sensory (like a Novocain injection), the muscles were fine.

Then less a week later at work, my lips and cheeks started twitching. My chin would start to quiver as if I were about to go on a crying jag. Because this was now muscular, I called the VA hospital in Seattle and told them I was on my way down.

I came in through the ER for my first treatment of solumedrol intravenous infusion, they lodged me out in a hotel, and I came back to the hospital for the next treatment in the IV Infusion room the next day, then back to the hotel to await my last treatment the next day.

It all went quite well. I was lucid, happy and talkative up until the last taxi ride to the hospital and by then, I just want to be home on my couch. Not exhausted, but just ready to be somewhere else.

The exhaustion comes next. After three days of solumedrol infusion, I go home with high doses of prednisone. My muscles are all drunk. It's the best way to describe it. The large leg muscles like my quadriceps and calves have no strength (hence the use of a cane) and I get tired very quickly.

I actually have no idea right now just how exhausted my body is because Paulie won't let me do anything. This past weekend I was allowed off the couch for potty breaks and one alarmingly exhausting shower.

I would stand up and teeter at the edge of the couch waiting to see if my body would allow me to step forward and I'd hear Paulie pipe up, "Where do you think you're going?" "I was just going to... then I was going to..." "I've got it, lie back down. Now." Sometimes he'd hear something fall or break in the other room and I'd hear him shout, "Go sit down!"

On Friday or Saturday (the days are all running together) he made the most brilliant barbeque beef in the slow cooker. He said when he got out of bed to go get it started, I said, "Goodbye", and when he came back a half an hour later I asked him where he went. It must have been Saturday. I think.

Now for the specifics: Wednesday in the ER the student nurse tried to get the IV rig in my arm. It was a bloodbath. The emergency room was quiet, and they had seated me in the hallway. The student nurse got the instructions "off camera" then came to get it inserted and tape it down (the rig stays in my arm for three days and the meds are just hooked up, infused, and disconnected). I can't remember her name because it was Vietnamese, but she was a quiet, little thing.

I pointed to "Old Faithful", the vein that can always give blood or take medicine. She uncovered, unboxed and unwrapped all of the paraphernalia while I just sat there reading (Sir Arthur Conan Doyle's *The Lost World*, 1912). She washed me down, put the tourniquet on and started poking. Then she connected the plunger of saline and tried to push it, but it wasn't working. And then I started bleeding. A lot. All down my arm, down to my wrist, and it was starting to puddle on the table. I actually had to move my book out of the way.

Her supervisor came by and caught my eye. I sent him off with an, "It's ok, she's doing fine," look and he walked away. Do you see the problem yet? She still had the tourniquet on me. You can't push saline with the tourniquet still on. It wasn't arterial blood with a pulse, but with the tourniquet on, and a big needle in my arm, the blood was flowing freely. She was very good though. She didn't panic. Then I got the meds (first batch), then I went off to the hotel for the night.

AJ (the taxi driver) got me back to the hospital the next day after Eileen served me French toast (she was the waitress in the local diner).

At the hospital I went up to 2E, the infusion room and just peeked my head in the door. Sheila, the LPN IV nurse said, "It's the Fireball lady!" Now, if a nurse recognizes you after only seeing you three times six months ago, then that is either very good or very, *very* bad. This was good.

Last time I had a relapse, I brought Atomic Fireball jawbreakers (to attempt to get rid of the horrible taste of the solumedrol) and I shared them with the other people in the IV room. Hence forth, I'm known as the Fireball Lady.

Although this time I brought chocolate and bubbles. I pulled the bubbles out when no one was looking and started blowing streams of them into the air. The old guy next to me said to Marcia, the RN IV nurse, "Uh, can anyone *else* see those?"

It was truly an awesome moment.

I know that every time I speak of the VA hospital I speak with reverence. Friends would like me to see an MS specialist up here in Bellingham to avoid the four-hour round-trip drive, but until the VA starts treating me horribly, there is no way I wouldn't seek them out for help when I need them. It's hard to explain, but I'll try.

There's camaraderie in those halls that I haven't felt since I was actually in the service. There is no race, and no rank either, but there is something else. Honor. And no shame. The amputees, the blinded, the wheelchair-bound, the man wearing the hat that says WWII POW, the faded tattoos of lost glory, or gory, days, the broken bodies and still-strong spirits.

The posters on the walls from children, the quilts from the volunteers, the bronze statues and plaques, the free coffee from the local VFW. And the American flag flying outside. The thoughts are all there. We didn't die on the battlefields, but the sacrifice was still there. The saying goes, "We gave some; some gave all." We signed on the bottom line and handed our lives over to a government agency in order to protect the rights of fellow Americans and gave those fellow Americans the right to speak up and out, for or against anything they wish. We did that.

That's why I go down there. That's why I'm a proud veteran.

And then there's always a chance for me to harass the big guys. I dearly love all branches of the Armed Services, we are on the same team, but that doesn't take away any of the fun of a good ribbing.

I like taking on a Marine and saying something like, "So, you're ex-Navy, right?" He'd say, "No. I'm a Marine!" "But, you are aware that the Marine Corps is actually a small division in the Navy Department, right?" That's usually when they go find a seat somewhere else and I giggle and return to my book.

For the Army guys I tell them that there isn't anything you can do in any other service that you can't do in the Navy, and that there are things in the Navy that you can't do in any other service. "Oh, yeah? Name one." "Submarines." "Oh."

For the Air Force, I thank them for, in times of war, sending their officers out first (jets).

There's Coast Guard there too, and I think maybe even National Guard. All of us are on the same team.

If I'm not in the mood for good natured harassment about which of the Armed Forces is the best (NAVY NAVY NAVY), then I'll just choose a seat next to someone who looks lonely and reeks horrifically of pee and talk to them for an hour about the logo on their tee-shirt or a pet or whether they like Letterman, Leno or Lopez better.

That's all at the hospital, though. Now, I'm home. Yesterday I had double-vision, today my lips still quiver. Tomorrow? Who knows?

These are my adventures with MS.

" Ice Creamed"

Soon after my latest relapse, I was laid up on the couch with what I call "MS exhaustion." It's harmless and temporary, but decimates my physical power, balance and coordination, and I have to use a cane until I recover.

During this time, Paulie was waiting on me hand and foot shoving good food at me and changing the movie out whenever the end credits started rolling. I suggested a reward for both of us: maybe we should get some ice cream. He perked up right away (loves the stuff) and got a pad of paper to get my ice cream choice(s), hooked a pen on the pad, and threw it at me.

Now, I saw him throw it, and I saw it coming my way, but I knew this just wasn't going to end well.

It happened in slow motion. I could see the papers fluttering in the air, the flash of the clip on the pen, and the joy vanish from his face only to be replaced by horror as he realized there was no way I could get my arms up in time to block it, much less catch it. It clocked me solidly on the forehead and finished its flight over the sofa.

He got this, "Oh, crap" look on his face and said, "I'm going to pay for that when you get better, aren't I?" I said, "Oh, yeah," as I finally gave up the delayed struggle of defense and lowered my arms from their weak attempts at reaching the zenith over my face.

He came back with four different flavors of ice cream, all half gallons. Huh, I guess it did end well after all.

"Fair Game"

Paulie and I wrestle hard. We throw down on the floor, on the couch, in the easy chairs, the cats run, we've tipped over food and drink, broke one of the beds at the Silver Lake cabins, ripped clothes, had food fights, water fights with spray bottles, crushed a house plant... the list goes on. I pull his leg hairs (not tug), he tickles me mercilessly and we both go after any bruises or sores the other might have. All is fair game, and a good poke dead center of a new abrasion can bring the big man down.

My point is, we are always on the defense with each other. He now knows that he can't wake up in the morning and rub the sleep out of his eyes because I will reach over and bonk his hand driving it into his eye. Why not? I'll even talk nice to him and wait for my moment. But once his eyes stop watering and he can see again, I know I'm in trouble. Hey, this is love.

He is also *ridiculously* ticklish. Fantastic.

A few days ago, he came home from work at 3am (late shift) and he comes up to bed to kiss me. I wrapped a blanket around myself and followed him to the top of the stairs.

He turned to look at me and said, "Where do you think you are going?"

I said I wanted to go downstairs and be with him when he ate his dinner and he instantly replied, "Oh, no you're not. You are way too unstable to go down those stairs just to watch me eat dinner."

I should mention that at this point in time, I'm smack-dab in the middle of an MS relapse and, consequently, I'm as weak as a kitten and exhaust easily.

And then he suddenly lunged at me... or so I thought. He probably just stepped forward to turn me around like a little kid and send me off to bed, but I thought, in my years of training with him, that we were going to wrestle.

I freaked out, braced my body and screamed like a little girl and then spun around…and ran right into the wall.

We laughed so hard we were actually screeching (I'm sure the neighbors have nightmares about us, it is three o'clock in the morning, after all).

I said, "I don't need you to wrestle with, I can kick my own ass, thank you."

He eventually helped me off the floor and made me go back to bed.

Yet another adventure for the books.

"Slow Learner"

Once after a relapse, I was showering and getting ready to go to the family's house for the Fourth of July barbeque.

Showering is exhausting. I've almost blacked out before, and this time I was actually getting nauseous and sweating: it's a real battle.

I'm thinking, do I really need to wash my hair? I pushed myself through and lathered up the washcloth and can just feel the water washing away ounces of precious battery power as it takes the soap from my body.

Then I'm thinking I should shave. It's just one more step. Just shut up and do it. So, I shaved. I was feeling stupid for pushing myself so hard, but it was done. Stubbornness won over illness. Woo hoo!

But, as I grabbed the towel bar and hauled myself out of the shower, I realized that I was completely spent. If this was the end of the task at hand, all would be well after a short rest on the couch.

But it wasn't over. I wasn't ready to go to the barbeque.

I was dripping water, overheated, and I was sweating and I desperately needed to lay down in the worst possible way and thought about the bathroom floor.

The tiny bathroom rugs looked ridiculously comfy at this point, and I could use the bath towel as a pillow, but Paulie would never forgive me if I didn't call for his help and just laid down right here. You think he coddles me now? If he saw how much I pushed myself this time then the next MS relapse he would bind me up like a mummy and never let me out of his sight.

So, I hung in there and made it, dripping wet, to the bed. Uh, his side of the bed was closest…

As I lay there, soaked with bath water (and sweating), gasping for air, I tried to get my exhausted, shaky muscles to calm down. Once I felt a little better, I got up and went back into the bathroom. All I could do was comb my hair, and then I was too exhausted again so

I went back into the bedroom and lay down on the now wet sheets (and I'm still dripping water because, at this point, drying off with a huge, heavy bath towel was just a dream).

After I regained my strength (and stubbornness) and went back in to brush my teeth. Exhausted, seeing black spots, and nauseous yet again I was also very, very shaky, I had to go back and lay down. Will I ever learn?

All this time I'm thinking of my poor sweet Paulie. I'm getting his side of the bed soaked. Awww.

Then I actually laughed out loud and thought, oh no. This is payback. He's tickled me so hard before that I've actually peed.

Once it was on him, but that was stress incontinence due to laughter (he made me laugh so hard that I peed my pants), his fault entirely, as I see it.

And it wasn't once, it was twice.

He too, is a slow learner.

"Veteran's Hospital"

From just a tiny patch of numbness on my left index fingertip four weeks ago this relapse of multiple sclerosis has spread to one-third of my torso with no end yet in sight, even after a hospital stay. It's a Novocain kind of sensation that includes temperature sensing changes and loss of muscular coordination and strength at my shoulder and wrist.

I am lucky and feel deeply grateful for many things. These past few days have shown me human kindness that humbles me.

As far as my illness goes, I still believe that I will have a full remission. Even if I don't, I am still grateful that the disease took my left arm, and not my dominate right. I am thankful that I can type, which won't interfere with my career. I am thankful that my brain didn't turn to mush. I am thankful it didn't take my legs, so I can still ride horses. And, I am thankful that I am not in any pain.

Any or all of this could still happen, it's a progressive disease which means that this is the best it will ever be, but now we are just trying to make the downhill slide less of a snowball effect and more of footnote.

As I understand it, some suspected causes are genetics and pollutants. A recent story in a reputable paper stated that Gulf War vets are now showing symptoms of both multiple sclerosis and amyotrophic lateral sclerosis (Lou Gehrig's disease).

This is a horrific thought to that new population, but one must have continued hope to discover a cause and find a cure to those already afflicted. My own father was a Vietnam veteran who was exposed to massive amounts of Agent Orange before I was conceived in 1968. I see this as a possible cause for my illness. I have documentation of his Agent Orange exposure.

As most of you already know, I'm not one to say, "Why me?"

The way I see it is, Why not me? I am human. I am fallible. I am weak. I can get sick. I can die just like everyone else out there.

I am not special with superhuman strength or any special powers. I am just more stubborn than the average bear.

And I have a wicked sense of humor.

So, just days ago I realized that this round, this relapse, this attack, wasn't getting any better and gutting it out wasn't going to fix the spreading numbness. I needed help. I called the designated number at the VA and left a message. A doctor called me back and agreed that I needed to come in right away for treatment, but she wanted to get concurrence from the chief resident neurosurgeon, so he called me back an hour later and said that I needed to come down as soon as possible. Plans were being rushed to get me in, and thinking I was going to go down there that same day, I left work to go home and pack and hit the road to the Seattle hospital one hundred miles away.

This was when I felt the first rush of human kindness. It took me awhile to extract myself from work because I was overwhelmed with friends and coworkers giving me their fondest wishes and kindest prayers.

Most didn't know of my affliction, and I had to calm their fears. Their questions were not nosy, mean spirited or gossip-making inquiries. They were kind people who cared.

I got home, packed, prepped the house, cats, and plants, shot off an email and waited for the doctor to call me again. When he did, he said that they couldn't get me in until early the next morning. Not a problem.

At the crack of dawn, I got up, tested my limbs, and jumped in the shower. When I tried to reach for the shampoo, I realized I missed the bottle by two inches. The relapse had progressed overnight; it now included compromised muscular strength and motor coordination instead of just being a sensory problem. This is big. And scary. It's my first brush with this part of MS.

Check-in was at noon, as was my first infusion treatment. As was lunch. I went to the treatment room and had the IV put in and got the solumedrol started. As soon as I was settled, the nurse said, "We have your lunch here, are you hungry?"

As I took the tray from her, I realized that the menu receipt was tagged with my name. It wasn't a generic lunch. The VA cafeteria had been informed that I was arriving that day and that at lunch time I was going to be in this treatment room. The menu had all of my particularities. I don't drink coffee; I drink hot chocolate. I don't drink apple juice; I prefer cranberry juice. Three years ago, during my very first visit, someone with a clipboard showed up at my bedside and said, "You have no diet restrictions. What do you like?" Three years later, I'm still in their computer. And I still like hot chocolate. Lunch was Turkey Tetrazzini and Broccoli Normandy. It was very good, but why anyone would serve Broccoli *Normandy* to a bunch of war veterans puzzles to me.

Once in my room I unpacked. My roommate was in for cancer, she'd been there for weeks, finishing up on some radiation. Next door was another woman, also in for cancer. She'd been there for nine months. I'm Navy, and my roommate was Air Force, but I liked her anyway.

While I was unpacking I realized that I should have brought my slippers after all. I decided against bringing them in favor of socks. That night, despite being up since the crack of dawn, I didn't get to sleep until about 4am and spent the night wandered through the halls of the hospital – in my socks.

I couldn't sleep for many reasons, but one of them, a big one, was that the pillows were like flat cinderblocks. Complaining to no one, I rose the next morning, made my bed, and padded down the hall barefoot to fetch another blanket for the following night.

Upon my return to my room there were three things sitting on the foot of my bed: a pair of hand quilted slippers, a soft neck roll pillow and a deck of cards.

Everyday a volunteer comes by with a cart of mostly homemade items to give to veterans to comfort them while they are in the hospital. For free.

Now, you know how touching the first two items were to me at that very moment, but as for the deck of cards... Giving a deck of cards to a McCulloch is about as magical as serving up Spam in Hawaii... I couldn't believe my good fortune.

Human kindness. I'm telling you that it exists.

Between treatments (I'd be there for three days), I walked the halls.

In the second day of walking I realized that these were halls were hallowed. The dictionary describes "hallowed" as showing respect or to honor greatly, to revere; highly venerated; sacrosanct. Some people save this word for the church or the temple or even a football or baseball field, soccer pitch or hockey rink, but for me, it's the halls of a veteran's hospital.

These men and women, on the orders of the President of the United States, their Commander and Chief, served and protected their country against all enemies, foreign and domestic.

These men were a part of history. They fought the Nazis. They were the ones flying high over Pearl Harbor and pulling their shipmates out of the wreckage. Iwa Jima. Korea. They were the ones in Vietnam. Panama. The Gulf. Iran. Iraq. Afghanistan. Africa. They protected embassies, our shores, our presidents. They were on the early submarines, the ancient planes, the long forgotten flat-top ships, they were Calvary although the horses were a thing of the past. They marched on their own two legs, sometimes carrying the sick or the dead. The jungles. The snow. The deserts. The trenches. Under water. In the skies. Most volunteered. Some were drafted. Those who were drafted and served their country walk these halls, their bodies are broken, their minds dark. But they still served.

Most of the men I saw were accompanied by wives. Most were probably their second or third wives, but nonetheless, these women were by their sides. Some of those women could have been the sweethearts left behind as their men went off to war, did another tour, went off on maneuvers, went on duty, went underway for six months or more on a ship. They could have been the women left behind to have babies by themselves, raise children in the absence of their husbands and moved from duty station to duty station for however long or for however far their husband's careers took them.

As for the women vets... Well, there are fewer of us around. And for as many women vets as I have met during my time at the VA hospital over the years, I have never met a husband or a sweetie. My own husband is the only one I have ever seen in any of the women's rooms, and he himself is a veteran.

As I walked these halls, I read the plaques, looked at the pictures on the wall, studied the statues and the flags and enjoyed the artwork of school children who praised their veterans.

This place cares for the veterans. Here they are loved. Here they are honored. Here they are sick and asking of help. Here they are safe.

Upon my return home my friends brought me food, flowers, cards and best wishes for a speedy recovery.

Human kindness.

I am humbled.

I am lucky.

I am loved.

"Switching Meds"

After eight years on Copaxone, a daily subcutaneous injection, I have opted for Avonex, a once-a-week intramuscular injection. It is interferon 1a, and fairly nasty stuff, which is why I've declined it for so long.

You could go on line, read drug books or the package inserts, but you never really know ahead of time how a medicine is going to react in your own body. It's no longer a statistic, it's you.

This one was interesting. For the first four hours after injection, I could not get warm. I wasn't shivering and Paulie said my feet weren't cold, but nothing worked to raise my thermostat. Except for the next two hours where I couldn't cool off. I wasn't sweating, but felt tremendously overheated. Weirdness. Adventures in pharmacology.

Although I am professionally trained on injections and phlebotomy, and have done thousands of subcutaneous injections on myself, I was not able to stab myself with the longer, bigger gauged intramuscular needle.

Paulie had no trouble.

Last Saturday was my first dose and before he slammed it into my thigh I said, "Wait. Wait! Stop!"

He had the dripping needle in one hand and eye contact on the swatch of skin he had just sanitized. He blinked and said, "Huh? What?"

I said, "Just do one thing for me first, ok?"

"Uh. Yeah. Sure. What?"

"Could you wipe that grin off of your face?"

Because of the bizarre and unpredictable side-effect, Paulie injects me Friday night after work and I sink into discomfort that becomes pain that lasts into Saturday and even, occasionally deep into Sunday morning.

Some of the symptoms I experience are extreme headaches,

extreme temperature fluctuations, extreme neck and lower back pain, congested "wet" lungs, and swollen joints like knees and knuckles, and lethargy.

I've try to read or go online but it's pretty futile. This is when I'm happy that we have a library of 1,450 DVDs. It's a collection that works, you know? A collection of tea cups or antique clocks really would not be helping me at a time like this.

For these movie marathons, Paulie's usually there when the end credits roll, and if I'm not asleep, he'll ask what I want to watch next. What a man.

Twenty-four to thirty-six hours later, I rebound quickly, if that makes any sense.

Case-in-point: when we were watching football on Sunday, I was continuing my huddle in the easy chair and Paulie was quietly resting full-length on the couch.

During halftime I got up, threw off my blankets, ran around the coffee table and launched myself into the air at him.

After the screaming stopped, he said, "I guess you're feeling better."

I said, "Oh, yeah. Sorry. I should have mentioned that first, huh?"

"No problem," he said, "I figured it out in time."

These are the side effects of living with me.

A week or two passes…

This past weekend brought on a new experience with my new treatment. Violent shivers.

Paulie gave me the injection when he came home from work early Saturday morning. I was still in bed and we both went to sleep. Shortly after that, I woke up freezing. Then it got kicked up to feeling like I just fell through the ice. I moved over to my sleeping husband's body and convulsed over and over again.

He got up, pulled the blankets off the bed, came around behind me and covered me in heat. We spooned, while he sweated and I went on shivering.

Eventually, things calmed down to just a deep freeze and we went down stairs where I shivered in the easy chair.

Much later, I said, "I can feel warmth returning to my body – it's over."

He looked at the clock, "Eight hours."

Nine months later...

My injection on Friday was one of the worst ever. Well, the side-effects anyway. Crippling, horrible pain. Freezing cold. Hours and hours. I took 1,000mg of Tylenol, then another thou six hours later. It didn't help much, or if it did then without it I would have been screaming. This is not an exaggeration.

Saturday morning came about and I hadn't slept, and I was still in relative agony watching the hours ticked by. I thought about calling to cancel the appointment I had that day, but I had already moved it from last weekend.

I started thinking, "Wake Paulie up, and have him come with you."

Then it was, "Wake Paulie up. See if he'll go instead of you."

Then, "Just shut up and do it, dammit. Get up and go! Get it done! You'll feel much better once the appointment's over, and you've got the four new tires, and all will be right with the world."

I showed up early, hoping to get in and out quickly.

The first problem was that I had ordered 17" tires, but they saved 16" tires instead. I showed them the exact part number I called about: this was their error.

In pain, I waited.

Then the guy wanted to give me the 17" in stock (these were premium tires, better than the ones I asked for) at the 16" quote to appease for their mistake. I said okay.

Then they took off my tires, and put on the new ones.

Then the manager said no to the new quote.

Then they took off the new tires and put on my crappy old ones.

"We've ordered our tires, they'll be here Monday."

I could have stayed in bed.

When I came home, took more Tylenol and crawled back under the covers, I decided to go off the Avonex and go back to Copaxone. I have previously discussed this with my neurologist and have been authorized to switch back if I feel the need.

I felt the need.

It's been a miserable, horrible nine months, capped off by this latest relapse (the next story) that I have been unable to recover from so far.

There is still hope for that though.

Fingers crossed.

"MS 2011"

I'm out of here.

I'm having an MS relapse that started out four days ago in my right quad. I thought it would go away, but it's been spreading and this morning I called the VA hospital in Seattle.

I've now got numbness down my leg and up my back. It hit my right deltoid half an hour ago and I am now feeling my stubborn Irish dimpled chin tingle. It has never traveled so fast in my entire life. Frightful.

Days later...

Weak.

I'm not hungry but I'm forcing food and fluids.

Paulie made a pot of turkey soup, so I should try a spot of that today. Flavor's off, so everything tastes as if it's been boiled in pennies.

I'm bathing and putting on fresh clothes everyday which doesn't sound like much, but when you barely want to move, or can barely move without exhaustion, this is huge.

I do need to report that Paulie's very happy that I can't defend myself. He'll wait until there's a bed, couch or chair behind me, and then he'll point two fingers to my chest and tap me over.

This is usually after I've struggled to get to my feet and have someplace I need to go. Ass over teakettle. After the giggling stops, I warn him that I won't always be so weak and that I will avenge this misdeed and he will pay dearly. By this time, I'm usually on my feet again and that's when he taps me over again. Dammit.

More later...

I didn't shower yesterday.

I know that you don't really need to know this, but if you think of it technically, like I do, you'd see it as a yardstick to how well I'm feeling.

I set little things up for me to push myself to do and yesterday it was removing my summer polish from my toes and calling into work to start my short term disability. I accomplished both, but was so exhausted the rest of the day that I never showered. And there was a small kitchen fire, but that was late last night. I wanted eggs and Paulie was at work.

What I'm looking for now is for me to be interested in cleaning and organizing my house.

Paulie's doing laundry, grocery shopping, cooking, working and cleaning house, but there are little stacks of stuff and little chores that need to be done like cleaning Buck's box or watering the plants or putting away my overnight bag that's still on the floor from the hospital.

These bother me as they would any other day, but right now I just don't give a crap. The day I do is the day I start feeling better. It's always been a direct mirror on my psyche whether it's the flu, major depression, sinus headache or an MS relapse: inside equals outside.

That's why the missed tub-time was so disturbing. I like my body to be clean and not giving a crap about bathing a day is upsetting. I must have pushed myself too far.

Removing toenail polish = too far. Dammit.

More later…

Today is the first tapering down of the prednisone from 60mg to 50mg, there will be another drop in three days, then three days after that, until I'm down to one 10mg pill.

My planned return to work day is the 21st. As soon as the meds taper, I should be gaining strength.

But then I have my regular Friday night Avonex injection and that will put me down for a day or two. But then I'll start feeling better.

Today I plan on cleaning Buck the Guinea Pig's box. Very easy to do. And bathing. No matter what.

113

Oh yeah, at about two this morning I decided I wanted poached eggs on buttered toast with some bacon and a slice of tomato. It's very, very easy and quick to make.

The hard part was convincing myself that it was worth the energy to go downstairs. That took about forty-five minutes. I pushed myself.

The bacon was already made, so I sunk the bread in the toaster, and put the poaching pan on the stove, filled with water and cranked the heat.

When I was cracking the eggs into the cups, the flames came up over the shallow pan sides. Something in the drip pan under the electric eye had caught.

I moved the pan, turned off the burner and gently poured water over the fire, making sure I didn't splash any possible grease spill. The fire went out.

I finished making the eggs, put them on top of buttered toast and heated bacon and crawled with the food upstairs. I forgot the slice of tomato.

I ate with trepidation and slept with one eye on the cats thinking that they'd try to warn me (like Lassie) if there was a reflash in the kitchen below.

Nothing.

I was exhausted and clocked out.

Paulie came home hours later, "What's that horrid smell?"

No damage.

All is well.

And now for my 50mg...

Despite voracious eating, I've lost five pounds.

Not really hungry, but feeling an odd need to eat, I've been jamming down tons of food (far, far more than I could normally tolerate with my Lap Band).

Paulie's kept the fridge stocked with stuff I could quickly heat up and get back to my chair with.

I've been eating homemade burritos so I can cram down beans, meat, lettuce, tomatoes, and cheese; homemade nachos so I can eat salsa, and sour cream; his homemade turkey soup for the broth, turkey chunks, carrots, celery and noodles; poached eggs on toast;

frozen pizza; a pot of mashed potatoes; cereal; ice cream; homemade choc chip cookies; two bags of candy corn.

Lost six pounds.

Still weak.

I imagine now that there is a war going on in my body. The inflammation in my brain is fighting against the medicine sent in to tamp it down.

Mercifully, I feel no pain and haven't this whole time.

Today's Friday, I think, so it's been a week and a day. I still expect a full remission. I'll get there.

I break out in a sweat just brushing my teeth, but I'll get better soon.

I told Paulie I wanted to go outside.

He said no.

I told Paulie I wanted to go grocery shopping.

He said no.

I told Paulie I wanted to go see a movie.

He said no.

"And why not? I'm sick of being sick!"

He pointed two fingers, tapped my sternum and down I went. He caught me before I hit the ground.

"You're still too weak."

"But…"

"The answer is still no. Now, go lie down."

To be fair, the man has seen me take myself out without his assistance whatsoever. I'll suddenly have to grab ahold of something because my foot dragged when I was trying to turn around and I would fall if I didn't catch something quick.

Or, I'd just tip over. I think I'm going one way (usually forward), when actually I'm going another (usually backward) and have to windmill my arms frantically to regain my composure. Then I'll say something like, "Uh, you didn't just see that did you?"

"Yes, it was quite funny."

Dammit.

Sulking in my chair midafternoon yesterday, I felt particularly parched: unquenchable and icky sticky all day.

I was just about to reiterate to Nurse Ratchet how much better I was feeling when my upper lip stuck to my front teeth.

Oh, holy crap. It's more than just medicinal dry mouth. I forgot to brush my teeth. Ewww is right.

And now there's no way I can claim to be feeling better if I can't even do something I normally do without thinking about it. How can you forget to brush your own teeth? Ewww.

So, I pulled myself together in the last part of the day and finally cleaned Buck's box.

Then I brushed my teeth, showered, shaved… and brushed my teeth again.

Me: Sweaty, winded, seeing black spots and exhausted to the marrow of my bones, slogging back to my chair to recover from too much movement.

Him: My Superman cleaned the whole house, vacuumed, did laundry, changed the sheets and grilled pork chops for dinner. Sometimes, nurses can be very nice.

This'll be my last MS update; I'm sure you've all had your fill.

I go back to work on Friday (I'm eagerly looking forward to it), so I'll spend these next few days coming out of the medicinal fog and attempt to regain my strength.

Paulie scraped me out of my chair and we went on a Sunday drive after football. It was my first time outside in more than a week.

His team to win (Jaguars) lost; his team to lose (49ers) won.

My team to win (Patriots) won; my team to lose (Cowboys) lost - and they managed to do that feat in the very same game! They probably did it because I'm sick and knew I couldn't possibly stay fully conscience for two whole games!

So, the day was truly fantastic, at least for me.

I taper off again on the medicine tomorrow, then again two days later, and then shortly after that, I'll be done with it.

I guess that wasn't my last MS update; I'm not recovering like I did in the past. Now that I've used my leg a little, and am mostly out of the drug-induced padded fog, I can see that this isn't a full remission.

My entire right leg is still compromised, specifically, my right quad, side of calf and underside of foot. I also feel sensation and muscular changes in my right arm. I don't know about a possible weaker arm/shoulder/back/hip problem, but my leg is definitely "off".

This is all exclusively on the right side of my body (this mirrors my first relapse in 2002 - I've never had a "duplicate" symptom before).

I actually feel just as bad as I did when I walked into the VA for treatment a week ago, the only change is, it's not advancing anymore. But it hasn't dimmed in the least. This relapse is behaving differently than any I've ever had.

Traditionally, all symptoms of a relapse are gone by now. It may still leave me, but with the drugs almost done, it'd take my own body to repair it and I don't know if it will.

A limp is no big deal. I'll work with my doctor and maybe get some physical therapy or see what's next. Let's just wait a week or so to see what my body will do with it.

Either way, I'm lucky and happy and fortunate.

I went to work on Friday, but they sent me back home because I didn't have a return to work letter from my doctor.

The doctor thinks it's too early for me to work and so does Paulie. It was just a surprise to be kicked out of the office. That's a new one. The good news there is, my coworkers were very happy to see me and missed me, so all is well.

Today is my last dose of the meds and I hope to hear from my doctor on Monday with the new game plan. I am asking for physical therapy as I think it will do a lot of good and I'm pretty sure that there's no drug out there that will return my body to 100%. This is just the way it's going to be, and I'm fine with that. Life goes on.

I spoke with my neurologist today. She agreed on me returning to week for two hours per day this week, starting tomorrow, then four hours per day the following week, then six hours the following week, then full time the week after that.

My boss will probably have to kick me out every day because I'll "feel fine" and push it.

Also, an MRI is planned. And she's looking into physical therapy and occupational therapy.

She has also suggested that it could take up to six months after the relapse for the body to recover from any damage occurring during a flair-up.

All good hopes there.

Today, I pushed myself on the treadmill, and will continue that. Plus, Mom suggested crocheting, which is a really good idea because my handwriting has become loopier and bigger. Working those smaller muscles while crocheting is a good way to bring that around.

All is well; I have found the six pounds I lost this month, plus uh, three more. Paulie couldn't be more pleased.

"Stop laughing you mangy bastard. I'm almost up to full power once again, and am nearly ready to kick your butt!"

I was feeling rather gaunt and weak, now the steroids have puffed me out. I'm fluffy and my face is puckered and unhappy. That'll go away soon, no doubt.

Another side effect of the steroids is a weakened immune system. I had a scratch on my ear that got infected. I couldn't see it directly, but Nurse Ratchet peaked in there and said, "Uh, you better go see the doctor about this."

Before the first dose of antibiotics kicked in, I could that see a severely red inner ear become a severely red outer ear and everything crust over with pus.

This is not my favorite month.

I am stronger now, and have ditched the cane.

Buck's box is clean; the two dead fish have been scooped out of the tank and the tank has been cleaned, much to the delight of the remaining eight fish (carnivores, I would imagine); my checkbook is balanced; and a plant that needed to be repotted has been repotted.

My to-do list has shrunk back down to a manageable number of items and all appears to be back on track.

I plan on pushing myself, effort-wise, on the treadmill again, once I'm off the antibiotics for the ear-pus-incident, and once today's weekly injection of Avonex's side effects subsides, and that should help strengthen me more.

I'm still on limited duty at work. Two hours per day this week, but will start four hours per day on Monday, then six hours the following week, then full time again.

Smart doctor for putting me on limited duty at work. I'm exhausted far beyond what my iron will could handle.

Getting better. Getting better. I'm ready for a brand new month, though, let me tell you!

Gimping along. I've ditched the cane but brought it back for trips that are of an unknown length, especially if there are no rest periods (grocery shopping use the cane; work no cane).

I start physical therapy in a few days. Without the cane, I waddle (step, tilt, heave right leg, step, tilt, heave right leg – which turns into what could only be called a waddle). At home, I've discovered I still wall walk (I run my fingers along the hallway walls to be sure there's something there in case I misstep).

Fortunately, I have a very dark sense of humor so when someone calls me (jokingly) a gimp, I laugh because I honestly think that's funny as hell. Paulie called me something the other day (jokingly), then his face fell, "Oh, I'm so sorry." I said, honestly, "Don't be. That was funny!"

A friend told me that she doesn't know how I do it. She said, "If it were me, I'd be mad as hell and grumpy. You definitely look at the brighter side of things."

No pain. If there were pain, I would be a completely different person. That's just one of the reasons I repeatedly say, "I am lucky."

MS can have excruciating relapses. So far, none for me.

Actually, it's the weekly medicine that causes pain, but still worth it. There I'm lucky because I have the medicine. It's atrociously expensive, but because I'm a veteran going to the VA, it's just a copay.

Add to this, I have a job where I can go on short-term disability and disappear for weeks at a time when I have a relapse.

Lucky.

And grateful…

I had my first physical therapy session tonight after work. I walked in, and limped out in pain. My poor freaked out body.

After a thorough interview and testing, she had me on my left side on the table and told me to bend my legs, keep my feet hinged together, and then open up my knees, like opening a clam.

"Well, that was easy. What else have you got?"

"No. You shifted your body. Realign your shoulders, hips and left ankle like I just had it and try again."

Folks, I could barely lift my knee a few inches, and the next try after that it wasn't even an inch. That's the pathway that was damaged. One of them, anyway. _ab_

She said, "That's one of your abductor muscles, and it's not working so well. Your body is trying to get around it by shifting, like you just did a minute ago, and powering through to get the same result. It's not the best result, which is why you fatigue so easily. What I'd like you to do is regrow that failed pathway as much as possible."

I agreed with everything we spoke about, and she understood everything I was trying to say. This is a rare. She made a list of five exercises, including the one I just mentioned, and on my request, one stretch. Each of these I'm only allowed to do five repetitions - even the stretch! I begged for more, but she said that more is not better in this case, especially _if you can't recover from them within two hours._ I was about ready to call bullshit on her (two hours?!?), but with the pain I'm feeling now, I completely agree.

It's time for a hot bath.

Before I left, and before the pain sunk in, I asked her if she thought I should keep using the cane. When she said that she would like me use it, I was mystified. But now I'm thinking, "Duh!" and "Ouch!" and "Skip the bath and go to bed."

I wish Paulie was here so I could get a hug.

A year's gone by now. I never recovered.

MS 2011 will be with me the rest of my life.

Still, life goes on.

"Crunchy Ketchup"

My brain is fairly fried on some days.

I have trouble thinking of words, or even the name of a person I've worked with for six years – even as I'm looking right at her. Sometimes I have trouble saying words, and kind of stutter through a sentence. It's fuzzy logic, to be sure.

Often times I replace words that I want to say with words that I wasn't even thinking about. Like this morning…

Paulie was home from work getting his dinner, and I was up for work fixing my lunch. A PB & J. Easy enough.

When he was over by the cupboard, I said, "Will you hand me the crunchy ketchup, please?"

No response, so I asked it again, "Will you hand me the crunchy ketchup?"

Still nothing, and then he walked away.

"Why didn't you hand me the crunchy ket… oh dammit!"

He thought I was trying to be funny, and I thought he was being a moron, "Why won't my husband hand me the crunchy ketchup?!?"

After we stopped laughing, I said, "No, I'll get it," then went off to get the crunchy peanut butter.

Far better with strawberry preserves than crunchy ketchup.

And that's my morning.

Moroning.

So, my world now contains crunchy ketchup as well as a blue handicap parking placard hanging off my rearview mirror.

The reality is I have a brand new symptom that my neurologist calls *fatigable weakness*. My energy is depleted, and only gets worse when I move. I've stopped doing simple things like wearing makeup. That sounds small and stupid, but it's quite significant when you realize that that's something I've done most of my life and doesn't take but fifteen minutes to apply, and even less to remove. I also don't clean my house anymore. Or do laundry, or dishes. Or grocery shop or cook very much. Paulie is my champion, and if it weren't for him, my house (and life) would be a disaster. He has stepped up, taken over, and not complained once about his new burdens. Although I have often grieved about being unable to bare children, I realize now that if I had a full house, I'd have nothing to offer them. You can romance it all you'd like by trying to tell me that it would all work itself out if I had had kids, but I'm trying to tell you that I have houseplants dying because I don't have the energy *to water them.*

This condition is particularly brutal to my right side, where the last relapse presented itself. The muscles tire with usage at an exceptional rate. For example, when I do ten jumping jacks, it will feel like ten on the left, but fifty on the right. Once the power is depleted, it takes longer to recover. My dominate right is now weaker than my left. The symptoms looked like myasthenia gravis, but a blood test proved negative.

My energy starts out depleted, and only gets weaker.

Something as simple as a quick deep-knee bend to pick something up off the floor, or squatting for a second to choose a CD from the rack before bouncing back up actually traumatizes my right side.

My left leg would be like, "Oh, that felt good! Let's do ten, no, let's do twenty more!" and my right leg would be screaming, "What the *fuck* was that!?!" And for hours, maybe even a full day, my right leg would be jittery, spent, and delayed, which makes my limp even more pronounced. All of this drama from a movement that lasted less than ten seconds.

My right arm is the same way. If I carry groceries in from the carport, with the weight distributed evenly, my left arm would be fine, and my right arm would feel as if I just helped someone move a couch or a pool table.

I tried working out for five minutes a day, twice a day for week, and all went well.

The next week, I added five minutes, and things continued to do well with this *very* light workout routine.

The following week, I got twelve minutes into my warm-up and stretches before I suddenly felt my body shutting down.

It wasn't a faint. I have low blood pressure and sometimes see spots when I get up too fast, but everything gets better within seconds after this happens. This was *nothing* like that.

It was a full body shut down, like a computer crashing. And it didn't get better when I stopped exercising. My body continued to lose power, and I only had a few minutes to figure out what was happening, and that I couldn't pull out of it, and then call work to tell them I couldn't come in that day before I fell into bed and woke up hours later.

Six months later, I tried it again, and it happened exactly the same way.

Outwardly, I'm doing fine. I walk with a painful limp, and sometimes use a cane, but this other stuff no one ever sees.

Behind the scenes, though, it takes a lot to get there. I have a lot of help. I have an excellent neurologist and health care coverage. I have a great job with a company that has short-term disability, and I love my fellow UPSers: I work with amazing people.

I take a medication to fight the exhaustion, and an injection every day to try to keep the relapses few and far between. I have a speech pathologist, a physical therapist, an occupational therapist, and have done the neuropsychological testing that tracks the cognition problems. I get regular MRIs and consistently excellent treatment in the emergency room and IV Infusion room at the Veteran's Hospital.

I have great friends.

I have sincere family, including a beautiful, kind, loving, funny, generous, smart, attentive husband (and he's cute, too).

I have a jar of crunchy ketchup in my pantry.

Here's the thing: I know how lucky I am. My marriage, house, car, job and everything I've worked so hard for could be gone in an instant. My health could deteriorate into pain I've never heard of. Yes, it could be better, but it could be so very much worse. I know this.

I'm under no illusion that everything I've worked so hard for, for so long, can't be lost in an instant, or doomed in a cascade of trouble and pain, but I will always tell you this…

I am honored.

I am loved.

I am thankful.

I am so very, very grateful.

These stories are not about the challenges I face, but of the humor that gets me through them.

You just caught me on a good day.

…and now, I leave you with this…

"He-Man vs. Tripod Woman"

A few weekends ago, Paulie and I were out running errands. Because it's an indeterminate distance (in and out of stores, up and down isles), I use my cane to assist my weakened right leg.

After grocery shopping, while Paulie was heading off to the car to unload the cart, I veered to the right to go get myself a $5 smoothie at the health-food store.

Now, I don't go for the wheatgrass-topsoil version of smoothie that they offer there (along with vitamins, supplements, body-building powders and canisters of gluten-free protein *whatever* to make you look like you like to look at yourself in the mirror). I go for their strawberry-guava-banana-blueberry-frozen-fruit smoothie. Yummers.

Ok, now the key to this drink is, to get the most out of it, you need to drink it down just far enough so that when you get home you can throw a shot of rum into it. I definitely feel better after I have this amazing health-food drink. *It must be the fruit that makes me so perky.*

Needless to say, I'm looking forward to this drink, so quickly I waddle my way to the store and swing the door out (you know, as opposed to pushing it in) when I see someone in the store on their way out.

I immediately stopped the swinging door with my cane using the rubber bottom as a doorstop, and stepped aside to let him pass.

He was a twenty-something, healthy, well-muscled guy with a huge keg of muscle-maker-powder under each arm, and he'd stepped back to let me in.

I said, "Come on out."

His eyes got wide, he sealed his lips tight and he shook his head.

I said, "It's ok, I've got it, come on out."

He shook his head again. I said, "Really, I'm all right. Look, I'm a tripod. Come on out."

The look on his face and his body language was as if I had just told a hydrophobe to come on in, the water's fine.

Honestly, at this point, I was trying not to laugh. At him.

After the stand-off was over, I got my drink and laughed with Paulie all the way home.

And after adding a shot of rum for my Vitamin R, the story seemed to get much funnier.

It was a good weekend.

And now for some erotica

" Surprise Visit"

We are both exhausted, but I was the first one to make a move.

You are laying back on our bed when I move down your belly. You groan softly and push me away, but I say, "Let me do this." You quiet down and I continue on my way down your naked, waiting body.

When I get to your legs I spread them apart. You protest again, but I say, "I want to do this for you." You murmur something quietly.

I add some warm goo to my hands and move my body in between your legs so I can get comfortable and stay awhile if I want.

I look up to see your closed eyes. You are breathing deeply. You are relaxed. You are happy. When I look down, I see your full erection.

I pick you up, wrap my hand around you, and squeeze you from the base to the tip in one fluid movement, making sure that each of my four fingers runs right across the head. You actually gasp, and your breathing picks up considerably.

I look up and ask, "Do you want me to stop?" You shake your head and say, "No." "Are you sure? This is just one hand so far." You nod your head vigorously.

I wrap my other warm, lubed hand around you and push down, running my tight hand the length of your shaft. You know what's coming next and you start to moan and grab at the bed sheets.

Very lightly, barely touching skin, I run both hands up and down slowly and delicately. Your erection is sensitive and craving more than I am giving. You were hard seconds after I touched you and you want to quickly get to the finale while I'm still fucking with the opening scene. Gradually, I increase the friction and the speed until you are fully into it, then I slow down until your breathing slows down.

Leaning over you I open my soft, wet mouth and flick the head with my tongue. I can taste you. Lowering my lips, I suck gently just on the head. Warmth floods your groin as I cup and squeeze you gently. While I'm massaging you, I send you the rest of the way into my mouth until my face feels this tickle of your hair.

You are moaning rather loudly now and writhing on the bed.

I begin to pick up speed. You can feel the vibrations of my moan and feel the flicker of my tongue.

You suck in your breath as you feel yourself passing the point of no return. Rocking back on your heels you let out a scream as the first major wave hits you and then,

all of sudden...

you...

wake up.

Your eyes are wide open and you are sitting up on one elbow as your other hand travels down to your throbbing cock. You are confused and shocked to find that my head is down there and that you are still buried deep in my mouth.

And your orgasm is not done yet.

You fall back to the pillow and, sweating, finish the next eight or nine major waves before you are hammered with many small contractions and an almost instant hypersensitivity.

You flood me with drink.

I quickly finish and kiss your wilting erection before I fall down on the pillow next to you.

You are panting and trying to speak, but before you utter any intelligible words, your breathing slows and you go back to sleep.

$50 says you read it again...

And now for

a biography

&

an autobiography

"Biography: Marco & Polo"

I need to tell you about Marco and his twin sister Polo.

Marco was the sweetest, most gentle cat I've ever known. His way was soft. He was kind and peaceful and gorgeous. Sometimes when he would meow, he'd forget (or not care to) open his mouth. He was a friend to all.

Polo was beautiful. She was a riot, earning names like Bastress, Bitchy Smurf, Twisted Sister and Pandora. She opened her mouth often, and she wasn't sending out a sweet request, she was laying down an order. She was not the alpha cat, that honor went to my old girl Toby, but Polo had her staff…one adult male human being.

When I brought her and Marco home from the rescue as tiny babies, the little fluffs of hair tottered out of the cat carrier. While I just saw two black, long-haired kittens through the video camera viewfinder, Paulie said, "One of them is smaller than the other." Then he said something like, "The smaller one's got a little white on its chest."

He was doomed from then on out. Doomed, I tell you. The then unnamed, unsexed "smaller one" walked over to him, climbed up his shoe and promptly bit him on the ankle. She had chosen her man and there was no escape. She never grew too large for him to hold her in a single hand nor too heavy to ride on his shoulder (with her tail wrapped possessively around his neck).

From then on his ass was hers and she never once let him forget it. Every once in a while, she'd do what came to be known as her "lost kitten" routine. She'd start at the other end of the house calling out for Paulie like a momma cat looking for a wayward child and do a room-by-room search for him *at the top of her lungs*. When it became obvious she would go on and on, I would hear the bathroom door fly open and Paulie shout, "Dammit Polo! *You saw me come in here!*" She would then become instantly ecstatic and run, chirping and happy, to the bathroom, and the door would slam behind her, locking them in. Together.

Marco suddenly became violently ill. He declined so rapidly from a chubby, happy-go-lucky, brilliant little kitty to a deathly sick skeleton, that for several nights in a row, we would visit his sick bed and tell him that it was okay to go. He was so weak he couldn't walk nor could he even meow. He was so sick you couldn't comfort him with a petting, the most you could do was a gentle rub his belly. We thought of putting him to sleep. We dropped watered baby food and medicine down his throat for a week. We carried him with us, never leaving him alone except for work and at night when we said goodbye to him.

We loved him, we cared for him, and he got better. Slowly that little blessed being got stronger. Before he was out of the worst of it though, his fur, his black grown-out fur, turned gray. He then went from lying, to wobbling, to walking, to running to, once again, kicking his sister's ass. I am so thankful that we didn't give up. I am so thankful that he didn't give up. Later we did joke, however, that Polo probably had the same illness as Marco, but her evilness killed it off. Marco's fur, by the way, came back as fluffy and healthy and as black as ever.

Polo was a little brat sometimes. Most of the time, actually. But she always did everything so cutely that while you were cursing her out for her latest ploy, like the time she broke in to the maximum security, child-proofed cupboard full of freshly restocked toilet paper thirty minutes after its installation. You'd be softening up and thinking, "Wow, look at how pretty she is (with bits of toilet pap... *POLO!!!*)"

One of her favorite tricks was to run around the back yard, sort of to wind up, I guess, and then she would take off up a tree and onto the roof. No way to catch her, no way to coax her down. Paulie would have to climb up *and chase her on the roof* to get her back down the tree. We'd leave her up there, but she'd cry. Not to get down, mind you, but for the attention. We didn't want the neighbors to come knocking on the door telling us that there was some poor little kitty stuck up on our roof. The "cute" thing she'd do, the thing she'd do to soften you up, is pant. The tiny kitty up on the crest of the roof with solid black, glistening fur would have this itsy-bitsy pink tongue pulsating and panting like a big cat on the savannahs of Africa.

Marco was the only cat who could seriously mess with Polo. No one else would attempt such a deed. Twin brother could and would take her down. After a wrestling match of play fighting he would sometimes lie on top of her trapping her underneath. She would wail and cry as if someone had left her out in the rain. Marco would be calm, his head resting, eyes nearly closed, purring (though you had to get close to hear his purring over her caterwauling), he'd open his eyes if you ran into the room to see what had happened to Polo, then softly close them again.

Sometime after the twins second birthday we sat down to watch the videotape of their early kittenhood. We had guessed that Marco had become who he was because of his illness. We figured that because he was so very close to death, the trauma must have gentled him. Quieted him. Left him more reflective than reactive. Not so. He was born gentle. The film showed the two black fuzz balls being entertained on the couch. Marco played lovingly in Paulie's arms while Polo sat on Paulie's shoulder cleaning her crotch.

Despite Polo's self-centered ways, we accepted her shortcomings and *we loved her more because of them, not in spite of them*. I guess you'd have to say the same about Marco. His twice-kinked tail was, or would have been, a shortcoming to others, had we not chosen to bring him home for ourselves. We loved Marco more *because* of his flaw, not *in spite* of it.

Our sweet Marco died peacefully in his sleep at the young age of six. Our grief at his loss is still intense and heartbreaking. When we remember him, it's with a heavy heart. He always made us feel so good and so loved. It's laughter through tears when we speak of him. Saint Marco.

Only two years later…tragedy visited us again. Paulie, on his way to return DVDs before the midnight due date, heard Polo calling from the next apartment building over. He found her with her back broken lying under the stairwell. We presume she was struck by a car and pulled herself off the road. She was not mangled or bloody or crushed. Her eyes were bright and clear, and she was bitching up a storm, but her back legs didn't work. Paulie carried her home to me and I ripped the veterinary's card off the refrigerator, called and told them we were on our way.

When we arrived, the good doctor confirmed our fears, Paulie signed the paper and within minutes she was gone.

Polo was good and kind. A thoughtful, loving, generous cat who always gave the best… oh, no. Wait. That was Marco. Polo was a six-pound hellion, a regular Duchess of Darkness. She was a tiny thing with long silky black fur, big eyes, perfect ears and a little white "feather" on her chest which we presumed was her amulet, her source of power. She also had the loudest motor I've ever heard on a cat (must have been because of the zero body fat).

Later in life, Polo became a great Houdini because that little monster would do anything to escape, including launching herself off the second-floor balcony to freedom below. We built up the railing, but she would climb that, and then jump down. Most recently, she had gotten into the habit of torpedoing herself past our legs as we came home. She was not a social cat, so we had no fear of someone getting her, and she was smart and wary of cars, but this time her luck ran out.

In the pet hospital ER, after they had taken her back to examine her, I (oddly, if you don't know us), kept Paulie laughing. I would say things like, "Oh, holy crap. I bet Marco is probably saying, "Uh oh. I wasn't expecting you here for another 10 years. Party's over folks."" And when the tears would come back to his eyes, I tugged on his sleeve and said, "Can we get another kitten now?"

Eventually, though, it was time to grieve and let the tears fall.

Rest in peace, Polo. Give Marco our love when you see him. Mercifully, you were one of a kind but dammit, *we loved you deeply*, and you are dearly missed.

Both left us too soon, but our memories will keep them with us until we meet again.

"Autobiography: My"

I have lived a long life. I was born on a tropical island ten years after it became the fiftieth state and two months before man walked on the Moon. I learned to use chopsticks in Hong Kong. I bought a sapphire and diamond ring in Singapore. I walked through a sand storm in Saudi Arabia. I ate "steak" in Bahrain. I rode a camel in Hufof. I swam in the Mediterranean. I catamaraned the Persian Gulf. I rode in a helicopter in Texas. I saw the tapped rubber trees of Malaysia. I have ridden purebred Arabian horses whose lineage had never left the Kingdom of Saudi Arabia. I went clam digging with my grandparents at Pismo Beach. I fished the Rogue River with my father. I got my very first hangover in Cyprus at the age of 11 (it was the *Red Lady* wine). I missed the bombing of the B-Concourse of the Frankfurt Airport by one day. I rode a twenty-year-old elephant with a ten-year-old driver in India. I've been to the Golden Triangle and seen the Taj Mahal. I've seen the Eiffel Tower and the Tower of London. I've seen the Statue of David, the Sistine Chapel, the Coliseum, the Spanish Steps, the waters of Venice, the dirty city of Naples and the ruined city of Pompeii. I've seen Mona Lisa's smile. I took a drive down the Blue Ridge Parkway in the Smokey Mountains. I've heard the Harlem Boys Choir sing. I take pictures of the wind. I am a proud US Navy veteran. I've saluted the USS *Arizona* and the Wall. I've been a Grand Marshall on the lead float of the 4th of July parade in the town Ben Franklin founded. I became addicted to all things horse at the ripe age of 8. I won first prize for one of my photographic pieces in an inter-collegiate photo contest I entered when I was in high school. I danced with my sister in a disco in Tormolinos on the Costa del Sol of Spain. I shopped with my mother at Harrods. I had a very scary layover in Beirut. I rode a bike down the steepest paved road in the world on Mt. Hale'ak'ala, Maui. I learned that the object of this game is not only to do your best on your best day, but also to do your best on your worst day. *My hero is my step-dad.* I lived for part of a summer with a French family in Biarritz. I saw the beauty of the Alps in Switzerland. I was elected yearbook editor my senior year at the Grier School in central Pennsylvania. I've crossed the Mighty Mississippi and the Great Divide. I drank "Kickass Mason Jar Margaritas" at Bandito's on Oahu. I've picked blueberries in Massachusetts. I traveled around the world by myself at the age of 12. I was widowed at 23. I teach. I learn. I played hide-and-seek on our Navy's last diesel attack submarine after her decommissioning. I've seen Anne Frank's hideaway. I tossed a coin into the Fountain of Trevi. I slept in a monk's quarters in Rome. I walked the streets of the French Quarter. I carpool. I've twice toured Hearst's Castle. I consider myself to be a latitudinarian. I've seen the best of Canada, and the top of Mexico. I held a stingray in my arms and gave her a raspberry during a voyage in the Caribbean. I had a "bomb" in my suitcase at JFK and "alcohol" in my carry-on in Dhahran. I have MS. I've suffered a nine-hour layover in New York to get to Pennsylvania. I married my best friend. I've climbed Diamond Head. I've been told I'm a direct descendent of the sixth president John Quincy Adams through his mother, First Lady Abigail Smith Adams by way of my paternal grandmother, Dorothy Smith McCulloch. I worked in the convenience store in Marin County where Jerry bought his Cherry Garcia. I was a Visiting Angel. I've seen a world-class horse show at Madison Square Garden. I've chocked a Huey at sea. I took a picture of the Empire State Building between the Twin Towers as seen from the Hudson River. I introduced myself to Mohammad Ali because I was too shy to meet Tom Selleck. I sat for an evening in the same room as four US Presidents, directly behind, and only two rows back from George H. W. Bush. I taught deaf children how to ride and jump horses. I read to a blind woman. I cooked dinners for those living in an AIDS hospice. I love my mother. I finally understand my sister. I've been to Russia – technically. I'm an ARAMCO brat. I wore a brace on my legs when I was a toddler. I've been to Alcatraz during visiting hours. I crossed the Equator and the International Date Line before I was even a teenager. I donate my time and my money to the United Way. I learned how to drive a stick shift in a Bug. I saw Yul Brynner perform in *The King and I* and Sandy Duncan perform as

Peter Pan in Hollywood. I saw Olympic gold medalist Scott Hamilton do his back flip on ice. I've eaten alligator in Florida, lobster in Maine, and buffalo in Colorado. I have never eaten, nor will I ever eat, rocky mountain oysters. I've been to Dollywood in Pigeon Forge. I want to be a philanthropist when I grow up. I won second place for my Wedding Vow cookies in the Northwest Washington Fair. I am currently reading Cooper's *The Last of the Mohicans*, Asimov's *The Foundation Trilogy*, Bradley's *The Mists of Avalon*, DeMille's *Lions Game*, Michener's *Alaska* and I always have a Stephen King book going. I've looked through the window of the 6th floor Texas Book Depository. I circled the remains of the building before the memorial was built in Oklahoma City. I received a personal phone call from the MCPON (Master Chief Petty Officer of the Navy), the highest-ranking enlisted person in the Navy, thanking me for an opinion I wrote for *Navy Times*. I've been in Bob Barker's audience. I have never been a part of a "flash mob" (and I'm ok with that), I've trained as a firefighter in chemical, biological and radiological warfare, and shipboard team firefighting. I qualified in Advanced Lifesaving and Water Safety and lifeguarded at a summer camp for autistic kids. I put myself through college and graduated with honors. I recently became reacquainted with my father's widow. I've picked "Blackberrius northwestus" in my favorite town. I am a proud UPSer. I am a patented inventor. I wrote this book. This is my biography: I have lived a long life, but I have not yet lived a lifetime.

And now for some

brainstorming

(and wandering)

"Burton Gauged Breast Pump with Corresponding Nipple Selection (US Patent #7,311,106)"

Because it takes more effort to suckle milk from the breast than it does to suckle milk from a bottle nipple, a nursing baby is reluctant to return to the breast after being bottle-fed. This is called "nipple confusion." The baby has effectively weaned itself from the breast to the easier bottle feeding.

The Burton Gauged Breast Pump is a small modification to any current breast pump model, only adding a gauge that would measure the suction required to draw milk from the breast while the mother is expressing milk to a bottle for her baby.

This gauged number from the pump would then be matched to a correspondingly gauged bottle nipple that would require the same amount of suction to draw from the bottle as it did the breast allowing the baby to go from breast to bottle and back to breast with minimal distress thereby eliminating nipple confusion.

This idea permits a mother to wean her baby when she is ready to, and not when she must, due to separation after maternity leave is over. She can express milk for bottles during the day, and nurse her baby at night for as long as she wishes.

Babies benefit.

" Envy "

If You Envy, Envy Only One Thing: A Disabled Person's ESP

I once felt sorry for the social shunning that a person with an obvious disability experiences on a daily basis, but now I feel only envy, for they have a power that an average person does not have: *They can see into the human soul and perceive within seconds just how good of a being one is by the way others treat them.*

If someone has a deformity, or a difficulty with speech, or a physical handicap that can be detected by others then one knows whether or not the unimpaired one has a good and kindly soul, or a mean, unhappy soul far sooner than someone who appears "normal" can.

Those without this extra-sensory perception cannot see past what people want them to see, and even if they have the training to read people, they won't be as fast nor as certain as a man walking with a severe limp because one leg is shorter than the other. He would know the soul of the person laughing at him from behind, or slamming the door in front of him, just as he would know the soul of the person who approached him from behind to tell him he's dropped something, or of the person holding the door open for him even though the "normal" person knows it will take him longer to get to the door than it would take someone without his particular handicap.

This is worth envying.

"Mother Earth: Landfill Miners"

A November, 2008 article in Forbes Magazine stated that "trash is cash," meaning that, even in a recession, the waste management companies did well. But it also said that, with escalating usage of batteries, new sources lithium was dwindling.

This made me start thinking about landfills, and I came up with this...

I believe that there should be landfill miners.

I'd like to start a company who has teams, dressed in hazardous-material suits that start at one end of a landfill and push through to the other end sorting out paper, plastic, steel, glass, wood, and things that need to be further broken down before recycling.

Leaving the non-recyclables like disposable diapers behind on a much smaller pile, I foresee other companies lining up at the dump like piglets on a sow, all waiting to haul away what they are designed to break down and harvest from the compound junk like metals, glass and plastics from electronics. Hidden away are the elements including metals like gold, silver, copper, aluminum, lithium and tin.

The local, state or federal law enforcement gets any weapons and the coroner gets any human remains.

Improperly disposed batteries, oils, fuels, paints, aerosol cans, explosives, accelerants and the like, can now be properly seen to.

It takes mountains of rock to make a pound of platinum. Why not mine the mountains of trash to makes tons of recycled raw materials that can be used to make what we need again? Why go back to the mountain to harvest the aluminum when we have landfills full of it already? How is this mining any worse? What we need to start thinking about is: How is it better?

Even things that can be sterilized can be resold or auctioned. I arbore this thought and would label it well for others who feel this way, but many others would look for jewelry pulled from the rubbish, and see *that* as a gold mine.

And talk about a renewable resource – how long would it take to get through all of the landfills and dumps in the United States alone?

Also, what municipality, state or foreign country wouldn't want these teams to turn their dumps over and harvest everything they can, leaving behind a hill of whatever was unusable?

I would think there'd be a waiting list for these services.

If there aren't companies out there that can haul off machinery and break it down to reusable elements, then now's the time to create one.

If they do exist, then now's the time to support them.

Imagine how long it would take to exhaust this resource worldwide – and what a wonderful day that would be.

What if this idea opened up to the world, and country after country started mining their own landfills, recycling with they could, and doing proper disposal of what they couldn't, leaving behind a much smaller pile of garbage for future generations to decide what to do with?

According to a Modern Marvels episode aired on January 14, 2012 on the History Channel, half of all paper made in the United States is used to package and decorate consumables, and 41% of all trash is paper.

Go get it.

"Poetry & Opinion"

I usually take the stairs two at a time going up,
and all at the same time going down.

I see a lot of seagulls
When I'm searching for
Hawks and eagles.

Even birds of the sky have to learn how to fly.

I'd rather be curious than know it all.

Love many, trust few, and always paddle your own canoe.

Is it a beautiful flower wrought with thorns?
Or, is it thorns graced by a beautiful flower?
Or, is it just a beautiful rose: petals, stem, thorns and all?

I'm a good cook,
I don't smoke
&
I conserve energy like a mid-winter bear –
This body was bound to happen…

"Third Attempt"

It's like pulling the pin.
Relaxing the grip.
And being unable to throw it away.

It's like standing on the edge.
Leaning forward.
And instead being pushed by a breeze.

It's like swimming out.
Looking back.
Then looking down.

Aggression does not start wars; defense of it does.

Unopposed, one can invade country after country until one owns the world.

It's only when someone stands up to the aggression that a war is started. With this in mind, maybe sometimes, war *is* the answer.

The only other alternative is two aggressors going after something that neither of them own or have any rights to. But then, wouldn't what they want to possess have the right to stand up to them and defend itself? Wouldn't this, too, be *casus belli*?

The question now would be, are you on the side of the aggressor, or the defender?

The most depressing personal thought I've ever had: Does it take more strength to make your dreams come true, or to survive after they fail?

The glass is neither half-full nor half-empty; it's simply a half a glass.

If you love something, set it free. If it comes back to you, blah, blah, blah, gag, barf... oh, look! He came back!

"Silver Lake Chess"

Using a classic chess board and pieces that move in their traditional fashion, the following rules are for a version of chess I invented while playing games with my husband at the cabins at Silver Lake Park, Washington.

This version makes it more a more spontaneous and bloody game of attrition rather than the old way of outsmarting your opponent a dozen moves before you can finally call out "Checkmate!"

With a clear board:
1. Start with all pawns in correct spots.
2. Advance pawns until someone says "Silver Lake".
3. Every five moves after that, pull a piece out of bag and place all four (or both queens) on their correct spots on the board. The kings are always the last piece.
4. Play until the game's traditional conclusion.

"Whimsy & Generosity"

I want to live my life somewhere between an English garden and a Japanese garden.

Have you ever seen an English garden? It's very crowded and jammed with flora seemingly without any rhyme or reason. Have you ever seen a Japanese garden? It's sparse space with highly organized and severely placed objects, all with a purpose in mind. All for meditation and deep thought. One garden is cluttered, appearing aimless to me and without purpose, while the other garden is too strict and well thought out.

I want *humor* and *element* and *warmth* and *life* and *purpose* with unusual surprises of color and organized for uplifting emotion, whimsy and generosity and without having out-of-control or over-controlled ideas.

It's a garden and a life that affects the five senses; a garden and a life that moves me body, mind, and soul; a garden and a life where it's alright to put your feet in the water, pick flowers and gaze up at the skies.

" I Believe"

I believe
that god is
innate in all of us.

I believe
that religion is
a learned response.

I believe
in Mother Nature,
Father Time
and the Universe.

And now from

the "Spiral Cookbook"

"Kitchen Chowder"

1c	chopped clams with juice
1lb	bacon, diced
1	yellow onion, diced
8oz	fresh mushrooms, sliced or quartered
½c	sweet corn
1T	garlic, diced
8	red potatoes, diced
2T	flat or curly parsley, chopped
2c	milk
1c	light or heavy cream
1T	flour
1T	butter

- In soup pot, brown bacon and remove.
- In bacon grease, sauté onion and remove.
- Add potatoes, clam broth and one cup of water to pot.
- Simmer until potatoes are tender (about 15 minutes).
- Remove one cup of potatoes, mash them, and then return them to the pot.
- Separately, whisk cream and flour until completely smooth, and then add to pot with the milk. Boil until thickened (about 3 minutes).
- Stir in everything else and continue to stir until heated through.

This started out as a clam chowder recipe from a book until I accidently dumped the clam meat on the floor. Not knowing what else to do, I opened the fridge and just started adding ingredients to the pot. The next year, I added more stuff. I love it because it's more than just onion soup, corn chowder, cream of potato, cream of mushroom or simple clam chowder, it's a magnificent kitchen chowder. Plus, anything with a pound of bacon has got to be good!

"You're Sleeping Alone Tonight Salsa"

6 Roma tomatoes, seeded and diced
1 white onion, diced
½ shallot, diced
3 garlic cloves, diced
1 T cilantro, shredded
Pinch of sea salt

Toss, chill, serve.

Uncle Jim asked me to make salsa "like you did before" for his upcoming 4th of July barbeque, but "like before" was nearly ten years ago and had no memory of how I made it. I panicked and almost just bought a jar, but instead I made a quick list of tomato varieties and favorite onion flavors, and then chose from that list and bought everything fresh, hand diced it and tossed together.

The first exhale after one single bite gave it its name.

It was a complete success.

"Dry-Rubbed, Roasted, Crock-Potted Ribs"

Buy two racks of pork baby-back ribs, an onion of your choosing, and a bottle of your favorite barbeque sauce.

- Remove ribs from their packaging and sprinkle with all of your favorite savory spices from your spice rack. I use the following: cayenne, parsley, sage, thyme, garlic powder, onion salt, red pepper flakes, salt, plus whatever else I might like. I sprinkle rosemary in the bottom of the Crockpot (after I've sprayed the pot with non-stick spray), so that it will steam upwards on the ribs rather than adhere to them making an unpleasant bite. After you've sprinkled both sides of both slabs with herbs and spices, you can leave it or chose to rub it in.
- Place the slabs on foiled cookie sheets and broil (roast) until meat is darkened (on the outside) to your liking. This is appealing because Crockpotted meat can look anemic. Flip the slabs to do the other side. The meat inside is still raw.
- Leave the slabs whole or cut into halves. I cut them even further into singles (for Super Bowl parties) or two-rib bunches for lunch/dinner/freezer. For parties, take the whole Crockpot (near the end of its cooking) to the party, plug it in and step back. Honestly, I have no idea if these things freeze well: I've never experienced leftovers.

So far, you've removed from packaging, sprinkled, roasted, and cut...

- Throw into a suitable Crockpot on whatever setting you want and remove hours later when the meat is done and pulls away from the bone to your liking. Some like it so most of the meat stays on and has to be ripped off, some like it almost falling off the bone, and if you wait long enough, it will all fall off the bone. Suit yourself.

- Empty the whole bottle of barbeque sauce into the pot two hours into the cooking. Dice the onion and throw it in, and then rearrange the ribs so whatever was on top is now on the bottom.
- Check on it every hour or so after the three-hour mark to answer the meat-off-the-bone question.

Best cooked when there aren't any carnivores or cavemen in the house.

Good luck!

"Hot Chocolate No-Bake Cookies"

2c	sugar
½c	milk
1	stick of butter
1	packet (single serving) of hot cocoa
1t	vanilla
½c	crunchy peanut butter
3c	oats

Pinch of salt

- Bring to a gentle boil in a sauce pan the first four ingredients.
- Remove from heat and add last four ingredients.
- Let sit for 10 minutes so oatmeal can soak up some moisture.
- Drop by spoonful onto waxed paper to cool.
- If they don't set fast enough, they can be frozen.

For the hot cocoa, you could use milk- or dark-chocolate, and you could even use the one with marshmallows!

"Cranberry Sauce"

18oz	fresh cranberries (buy two bags, 12oz each, and then use a bag and a half per batch)
2c	sugar
½c	cranberry juice (any blend you wish)
½c	orange juice

- Combine all ingredients in a sauce pan.
- Stir over medium-high heat until berries pop and it starts to foam (about 10 minutes of continuous stirring at this high heat).
- That's all it takes: you're done!

Serve warm or refrigerate: it also freezes well.

This can be for more than a Thanksgiving Day turkey. It goes great with spiral baked ham, roast duck and maybe even a Christmas goose.

Don't leave home without it.

"Wedding Vow Cookies"

I've just been informed that my "Wedding Vow" cookies have won Second Place at the 2012 Northwest Washington Fair! *Woo hoo!*

Our wedding vows state that I have to make these for Paulie every year.

2c	flour
1c	ripe banana
2½	sticks of butter
2	eggs
¼c	honey
¾c	brown sugar
3	shakes of salt
1t	*each* cloves, nutmeg, allspice, cinnamon, vanilla, baking soda
1½c	chocolate chips
1½c	raisins
3c	oatmeal

- Combine all ingredients (oatmeal last).
- Let sit for 10 minutes so oatmeal can soak up some moisture.
- Tablespoon onto ungreased cookie sheets.
- Bake at 350 degrees for 13-15 minutes.

And now a branch from a tree

MY DAD, SCOTT SMITH MCCULLOCH, AND ME.

This is a family photo taken in Medford, Oregon in January, 1986. It was the last time I ever saw him, as he left this world on his own terms the following Christmas. I miss him dearly and have always wished he could have known me as an adult, rather than the 16-year-old girl seen here.

JENNIFER.

This is my favorite picture of my sister, Jennifer. I took it at my great-aunt Neva's chicken ranch in Porterville, California in 1985.

MY MOM, MARCIA, AND SADIE OUT FOR A RIDE.

This is my loving mother and her loyal dog, Sadie. I took this on a scorcher of a day on Lake Texoma, North Texas, in August, 2011.

MY STEP-DAD, BARRY, AND MY NEPHEW, TRAVIS.

This is a picture I took in Laguna Beach, California, of my beloved step-father and his first grandchild, in 1992. I call it, "Grandpa's First Steps."

And now from the

book "Shutterbug"

"Gandering the Goslings"

BELLINGHAM BAY FROM BOULEVARD PARK
BELLINGHAM WASHINGTON
JUNE 4, 2005

Kodak CX6330 Zoom Digital Camera (F/8, 1/125 Seconds)

I intentionally cropped the first and last gosling to give the impression that the line of goslings actually goes around the world.

Zander and her man.

On a logging road.

A BEAUTIFUL FALL DAY.

AN INTERRUPTED MEETING.

A BREAK ON A HIKE.

FLOWER IN THE GRASS AT LAKE SAMISH.

PURPLE THISTLE ON SUNSET POND.

DAISY ON THE ROADSIDE.

WATER DROPLETS.

INCREDIBLE BEAUTY AT MILE MARKER 38.

A PLACE CLOSE TO OUR HEARTS.

CAMOUFLAGED...

...BUT I STILL FOUND YOU.

MOLLY.

REFLECTION AT SILVER LAKE.

I took this photo looking down into the water's reflection of the horizon, and then I flipped the picture 180 degrees. I have never seen this technique before, so I am calling it my own.

In color, everything is in shades of gray, except for the yellow corona of sunlight.

A Study in Lines.

A Study in Water Movement.

And one final dedication

BARRY H. FUNK.

Dad,

I want to thank you for the wonderful life you provided for me. I do not believe I would be who I am or where I am right now if it weren't for you.

Your level head and sound heart provided and even keel for the three (very) cranky females you married into, and for that alone, I am grateful beyond measure.

Happy 75th birthday this year, Dad. I love you.

Daughter Julie

(Enter my full name and
hit enter). ;)

Rate my book on amazon.com.
(Enter my full name and
hit enter). :)